Willows by Flowing Streams:

Raising Children of Promise into Gospel Maturity

Willows by Flowing Streams:

Raising Children of Promise into Gospel Maturity

Dr. Robert Davis Smart

Willows by Flowing Streams:
Raising Children of Promise into Gospel Maturity

© Dr. Robert Davis Smart 2020

Published by
Lighthouse Christian Publishing
SAN 257-4330
5531 Dufferin Drive
Savage, Minnesota, 55378
United States of America

www.lighthousechristianpublishing.com

Table of Contents

Foreword

One of my earliest memories as a child is when my family lived in a seminary apartment in St. Louis. I was probably about four and had been caught in the kind of mischievous and rebellious wrongdoing typical of a boy my age. I was no stranger to the wooden spoon that doled out punishment in our home, so to delay the inevitable I had asked to use the restroom. Having returned from this, I sat on my father's knee in silent trepidation, awaiting judgment. As he patiently explained what I had done, that was wrong, and what about it was sinful, I distracted myself with details from the room around me: the square-ish red numbers of my parents' alarm clock, the fanciful pattern of the quilt, and melancholy gray of the light as it diffused through the bedroom curtains. Then, my attention snapped back into focus as I realized the tone and content of my father's words were veering off from the well-explored regions of sin and punishment into new territory – a region whose signpost read simply, "Mercy." Though we had both agreed on my guilt and though we both knew the penalty, instead of the spoon I found myself being warmly embraced and pronounced "forgiven." Startled, amazed, and grateful the only thought in my head I remember clearly is, "I love mercy!"

My fervent prayer for readers of this book is that they be empowered to find where Isaiah's promise of "willows by flowing streams" intersects with the nitty-gritty of their daily life as parents. It's all too easy to feel disillusioned with such promises in scripture when confronted with daily life in the "real" world. Where the demands of work, marriage, and housekeeping make it feel an achievement just to keep our children showered, fed and off to their respective activities. Where the hope of providing soul-flourishing care gets lost somewhere between the grocery store and the soccer field. My parents, Bob and Karen, certainly lived their lives in this same very real and broken world, but by the grace of God they chose to persevere and hold on to the promise of his Word.

In the age of the ebook and the blog we don't lack for opinions on the latest and greatest parenting techniques, but I firmly believe that there is no great secret to parenting. There is no 5-step process for success. Rather, my parents enjoy the blessing of all their children walking with the Lord because they choose to follow the ancient practice of simple faith in a real God. A faith put into practice through daily prayers to a merciful savior on our behalf. Therefore, I encourage you to emulate the "noble Bereans" (Acts 17:11) and to dig into this work with your bible open, discerning "whether these things are so." Cling to God's promises in faith that another generation may arise to say, "I love mercy!"

Nate Smart
Married to Leigh Ann with four children
Engineer & Elder at Riverside Church
St. Louis, Missouri

Introduction: Vision: Willows by Flowing Streams

For I will pour water on the thirsty land,
  and streams on the dry ground;
I will pour my Spirit upon your offspring,
  and my blessing on your descendants.
They shall spring up among the grass
  like willows by flowing streams.
This one will say, "I am the LORD's,"
  another will call on the name of Jacob,
and another will write on his hand, "The LORD's,"
  and name himself by the name of Israel. (Isaiah 43:3-5)[i]

Parents need vision, a picture of their children's future. The King James Version bible, Proverbs 29:18a, stated: "Where there is no vision, the people perish." God gave Karen and I a vision, a picture of our children's future many years ago through two families, one I did not even know and one we've known and loved.

The first was in a recruitment video of a family walking in a park together, a Christian family that attended the theological seminary I was considering at that time. Although I can't remember much about the content, I remember the image because it was a mature family of seven. The children were grown into Gospel maturity by table instructions and loving parents, who invested the Gospel into their children. I never knew this family, but the image still is sweet to my soul in shaping our vision. I longed for our family to look like. I had a vision, through the first picture, that our children would one day be tall, mature, and godly.

The second way our vision for parenting was shaped came was through a couple who discipled us in a life on life way of missional discipleship. Dave and Cathy Bowman loved Karen and I like their own children, and we caught more than Dave and Cathy taught. We watched how they raised their two daughters into Gospel maturity in the context of a campus ministry they led at Purdue University through the Navigators. They have remained our models for more than thirty years, from having young children to being grandparents and parents in law.

Young parents need vision, which is often veiled because of the tyranny of the urgent, busyness in the now, and a shortage of models to inspire. Recently, our family was celebrating a one-year-old birthday of our grandson on vacation. The room was filled with young parents and lots of children. We were all having fun, dancing and playing with each other. Both Karen and I experienced a deep sense of joy that night and throughout the week in seeing our children as parents committed to the Gospel. Later that week we had a family picture taken. When I saw that picture, I realized that God had fulfilled the vision He had given us many years ago. Karen and I were standing in the picture with tall, godly, and Gospel-mature children plus many grandchildren too. Our children were like *willows by flowing streams, raised into Gospel maturity,* and it began with a vision. Young parents need vision to make it over the long haul.

God loves to give Christian parents vivid pictures, visions, of their children's future from real life and also in the scriptures; of when they reach Gospel maturity. These biblical similes and metaphors motivate us how to parent towards a beautiful end – the fulfillment of a vision for our children.

One of these visions from scripture for our children is that they will become tall *willow trees by streams of living water* (Isaiah 44:2-5). Children raised into Gospel maturity, like willows, require flowing streams of living water to grow and flourish. The living water in this scriptural text, it refers to the Holy Spirit whom God promises to pour out on our children. The Bowman's taught us to pray this promise of God for our children.

No Christian parent is sufficient to raise a child to Gospel maturity apart from God's grace through Jesus Christ. It is not a matter of presuming your child will simply behave as you the Christian parent for the same reasons. Children will see our weakness soon enough, which is not an obstacle when we point them to the Father above and to Christ, who pours out His Spirit of adoption. The key is that parents and children make the best use of the means available; namely, the Gospel and the Holy Spirit. God speaks the Gospel concerning Christ to our minds and pours out the Holy Spirit into our hearts that we may delight in what we know of Christ. The Gospel is the milk for a child to grow unto salvation and the meat for the mature Christian, but without the Holy Spirit there will be no growth or fruit. What is a *willow tree without flowing streams of living water* nearby? More is required than instruction and training in Christian behavior.

There such a thing as a psychological conversion, which makes a child appear to be a believer, but behavioral maturity without being ruled and fueled by the Gospel and the Holy Spirit is not the vivid and beautiful picture God sets forth in Isaiah 44:3-5. It is one thing for children of believers to own their parents' faith; it is another thing to merely own their parents' behavior. Something outside of Gospel parenting is required; namely, the Holy Spirit. God put forth this promise in His word, and in the visible word of baptism, that He will pour out the Holy Spirit into the thirsty lives of children – children of promise.[ii]

God has always had it on His heart from all eternity to glorify His Son in the outpourings of His Spirit upon all flesh, but particularly on believers' children's children. "I will pour out My Spirit on your offspring." On the day when Christ ascended, the Father gave Him the Spirit of Promise, and Jesus and the Father poured out the Spirit in great measure upon parents and their children. On that day of Pentecost Peter said, "the promise is for you, your children, and for all who are far off" (Acts 2:38-39). The promise repeated in the Old and New Testaments is for the children whose parents call on the Name of the Lord for salvation, and for peoples in every nation.

On the one hand, children must be born again and be indwelt with the presence of Christ through the Holy Spirit. On the other hand, they are raised into Gospel maturity by a constant, daily portion of the Gospel before and after conversion. Parents are vital for children, and therefore the aim of this book is to consider how parents may *raise their children into Gospel maturity* so that they may become like *willows by flowing streams*. Parents start with vision for their children.

To this end, then, chapter one addresses the need for parents to stay warmly present to their children in order to establish in them a solid sense of identity in Christ. This chapter unfolds the importance of establishing gender identity by honestly facing the glory, the ruin, and redemption of each gender. Essentially, God uses Christian parents to establish a solid sense of identity in Christ by an interpretation process of renouncing lies and speaking the Gospel into the hearts of their children.

Chapter two explains the implications of what it means that children are gifts from God, which fuels parents with gratitude for the children God gives them. Sometimes that means being thankful for a special needs child. It emphasizes how to dedicate children to the Lord, the significance of naming children, and what it may look like to trust God's promises on their behalf. This leads to the posture of parenting; namely, chapter three. In chapter three parents are somewhat raised by their children as God brings parents to their knees, to silence before God, to Gospel repentance, and to the school of wisdom.

Chapter four sheds biblical light on the nature of discipline. There are right and wrong ways to practice disciplining children, and it considers the three ways children tend to approach their parents. This chapter identifies the two primary questions children are asking their parents, different forms of discipline, the three weightiest character qualities to emphasize in discipline, and how to keep the bridge when children are unrepentant for a season. It also gives practical ways to teach children to play the second fiddle to other siblings, and ends with a call for parents to keep the bridge relationally with troubled teens and adult children.

Whereas the previous chapter was about the subject of discipline, chapter five is similar because the word *discipline* is like the word *discipleship*. Followers of Christ in the New Testament were disciples of Christ, and were first called *Christians* in Antioch (Acts 11:25). This chapter describes discipleship in the context of parenting – a life on life way of discipleship with an aim motivated by mission. It includes the matter of education, which covers all of life, reading, imagination, creation, sports, arts, language, scripture, catechism, theology, sanctification, sexuality, and maturity so that children may grow into Gospel maturity and become like *willows by flowing streams*.

In chapter six, like the previous chapter, involves all of life. It explains how parents mark their children's perspective of, and love for, God. It considers how to lead children in expressing their minds, affections, and wills to God in song, prayer, education, and work. Worship takes place in the home, church, and school. Worship is given to God and is expressed with our possessions and global concern that all the peoples of the earth give God glory.

An essential aspect of biblical parenting is found in chapter seven, helping children discern and fulfill their God-given callings. It shows the importance of seeing every calling in life as sacred, not just full-time vocational service as pastors or missionaries. This chapter puts forth a vision for the good life as an ordinary, weighty life lived under God's smile. It unfolds subjects like promoting differentiated leadership, cultivating compassionate service, appreciating the significance of prevocational jobs, and engaging in missions.

Finally, the last chapter unfolds a long-term vision for parenting. Chapter eight discusses what it means to cultivate friendships with adult children who have been *raised to Gospel maturity*. It is a chapter for parents to begin praying for future spouses or a call to singlehood, to walk children through engagement and their wedding days, to love and embrace the children in law God gives parents, and to parent in a fuller way; namely, to make a Gospel impact as grandparents in the lives of grandchildren. All this culminates for parents to leave a legacy from Christ to the next generation.

Questions and templates are provided for practical applications and personal intentions as a result of reading each chapter. This book may easily be used in a small group or discipleship settings in your local church or ministry context.

On a personal note, Karen and I do not see ourselves as experts. Rather, we have come to deeper convictions about the power of the Gospel and the Holy Spirit in parenting. God gave us a vision and the one in Isaiah as a promise to write about. We are always learning and regularly teaching about what it means for believing parents *to raise children to Gospel maturity*. By God's grace alone our children and children in law are like *willows by flowing streams*. Our children and children in law are filled with the Spirit, married, and are parents of our fourteen grandchildren. We have lived this book, and we share a burden for you parents, who are taking time to read and apply God's wisdom to do the same.

May the God of hope fill you with all joy and peace in believing, so that by the power of the Holy Spirit you may abound in hope as you read each chapter and apply it to your parenting and dear children of promise.

Discussion Questions

1. Is there an older family model in your life or picture that inspires you with a vision for your family's future? How does that vision relate to Isaiah 44:3-5?

2. How does the simile of the willow by flowing streams describe your vision for your children or child?

3. Why is the Holy Spirit vital for parents in raising a child into Gospel maturity?

4. As you read the summary of the chapters to come, which ones interest you the most at this point?

Chapter One: Staying Warmly Present to Establish Identity in Christ

Parenting is not for the faint of heart, but God will use your presence just by showing up. It is a calling from God, which flows from a Christian parent's Gospel identity and is invested in the next generation. This chapter aims to show the marvelous and significant calling parents have in giving children a sense of God's constant presence by staying warmly present to their children in order to establish the children's identity in Christ. How do parents give children both a sense of God's warm presence and a solid sense of their identity in Christ? We will begin with God – the Father, Son, and Holy Spirit.

Parents and God – the Father, Son, and Holy Spirit

When parents have the slightest conflict the littlest children will come and hug the legs of their parents wherever they are standing. Children have radar for parental conflict. Children know when their parents are happily united together and when they are in disagreement and divided, which makes them feel either secure or insecure. Every person, each child, was built to partake in God's divine nature – in the happy and unified way the Father, the Son, and the Holy Spirit love one another. Christian parents were made partakers of the divine nature, according to Peter's second letter. Peter wrote:

His divine power has granted to us all things that
pertain to life and godliness, through the
knowledge of Him who called us to His own glory
and excellence, by which He has granted to us His
precious and very great promises, so that through
them you may become partakers of His divine
nature, having escaped from the corruption that is
in the world because of sinful desire (2 Peter 1:3-
4).

In this way parents can reflect the way the Father, Son,
and Holy Spirit delight in one another; namely,
perichoresis.[iii] This is God's plan for us. Jesus prayed that
the oneness of this triune intimacy would be experienced
in His marriage to His bride – the church. Jesus asked,
"that they all may be one; as You, Father, are in Me, and I
in You, that they also may be one in us" (John17:21). A
parent's entering into this fellowship of love between the
three Persons of God is key to how their presence matters
to their child.

The 12th century reformer Bernard of Clairvaux spoke of
the Holy Spirit as the kiss of God, the Holy Spirit
proceeding from the love of the Father and the Son
through an act of their unified will. He wrote:

If, as is properly understood, the Father is he who
kisses, the Son he who is kissed, then it cannot be
wrong to see in the kiss the Holy Spirit, for he is
the imperturbable peace of the Father and the Son,
their unshakable bond, their undivided love, their
indivisible unity.[iv]

We were made to feel secure in this "unshakable bond" of "undivided love." Children cannot think of one parent without thinking of the other just as Christians cannot think of one person of God without the other two. For example, Gregory of Nazianzus (c.329-c. 389) wrote: "I cannot think of the One, but I am immediately surrounded with the splendor of the Three; nor can I clearly discover the Three, but I am suddenly carried back to the One."ᵛ Parents ought to share a united vision for their children by offering their teaming presence and eyes of love upon their children. Parents offer children fatherly love and support, Christ's sacrificial life of service, and the Holy Spirit's "kiss" of kindness and forgiveness when times are hard.

Each parent, both the father and the mother, will leave an indelible, mixed impression on their children, a positive one and a forgiven one. Giving children a sense of God's love in the context of community will leave a positive impression. The negative impression parents make on children is forgiven when the children experience consistent and loving presence.

This is true also for Single parents, who reflect God when they stay present to their children and Christian community, as Ruth and Naomi discovered when they were alone and lost their husbands. A child of divorce feels more secure when his primary parent is resting in a forgiving posture towards the parent living elsewhere. If divorced parents cooperate in mutual consent to order proper boundaries and a consistent schedule, then children can find security and sense all is at peace with God. The parent's presence reflects the Presence of God, and will enable the parent to establish a solid sense of identity in Christ.

Children need help from their parents how to interpret people and God in relation to their own sense of identity. Children are excellent observers, but poor interpreters. When children sense conflict or something wrong they tend to blame themselves for it. In my thirty years of pastoral experience with children of divorce, growing up in a single parent home, it is essential that children receive God's interpretation of their story. When there is painful separation in parents, children tend to blame themselves for it.

Since only one in five homes in the United States have a father present, it is likely that many readers are single moms. My thirty years of experience in working with children of divorce has convinced me that these children are very responsive to the Gospel, and willing to renounce Satan's lies about their identity. A single mother's relationship to God and a Gospel community is a perfect opportunity for the children to experience the love of God in three persons, and spiritual fathers are usually available to support these single mothers.

How is the knowledge of the trinity, revealed in the Gospel, useful for parenting? When Jonathan Edwards was a young student at Yale, he ruminated in his notebooks, "I used to think sometimes with myself, if such doctrines as those of the Trinity and decrees are true, yet what need was there of revealing them in the gospel? What good do they do towards the advancing [of]

Dr. Robert Davis Smart

holiness?" Years later, he wrote the answer to his question: "I know by experience how useful these doctrines be . . . for such doctrines as these are glorious inlets into the knowledge and view of the spiritual world, and the contemplation of the supreme things; the knowledge of which I have experienced how much it contributes to the betterment of the heart."[vi]

Parents reflect the love of the triune Persons of God in the way they raise their children, and they can enhance the environment and culture in their home. Just as God appears to His children in three persons in order to give us exalting thoughts and experiences of love in community, so the presence of parents offer their children their first taste of the Gospel. Enjoying God as one happy family of three, as it were, woos our children to long for the fullness of God in their lives. John Calvin wrote: "[God] so proclaims Himself the sole God as to offer Himself to be contemplated clearly in three Persons. Unless we grasp these, only the bare and empty name of God flits about in our brains, to the exclusion of the true God."[vii]

A mother was watching her son play with two other boys visiting. Each boy was competing to show that his father was the best. The mother couldn't help but listen to the conversation to hear what her son would say. The first boy said, "My dad knows the mayor," and the tension grew. The next boy said, "My dad knows the governor." The mother couldn't wait to hear what her son would say. Well, her son said, "My dad knows God." The mother smiled because it was true, and she knew every child wants to boast of this; namely, that his parents understand and know God (1 Corinthians 1:26-31).

Our calling as parents, particularly as fathers, is to point
our children to another Father, the Father they always
longed for. He says to His children, "You are my son or
daughter in whom I am well pleased." Consistent pointers
to find validation and favor from God makes for tall
willows by flowing streams, children less bent-over to the
parents or peers for validation. Jonathan Edwards spoke
of this in a sermon, saying:

> God is the highest good of the reasonable creature.
> The enjoyment of him is our proper; and is the
> only happiness with which our souls can be
> satisfied. To go to heaven, fully to enjoy God, is
> infinitely better than the most pleasant
> accommodations here. Better than fathers and
> mothers, husbands, wives, or children, or the
> company of any, or all earthly friends. These are
> but shadows; but the enjoyment of God is the
> substance. These are but scattered beams; but
> God is the sun. These are but streams; but God is
> the fountain. These are but drops, but God is the
> ocean.[viii]

In a way, every parent must be a broken idol, which
points children above to find their worth in the crucified
Savior and the experience of Christ's deep and wide love
through the Holy Spirit.[ix] As Edith Schaeffer put it, "A
Christian family is a mobile blown by the gentle breeze of
the Holy Spirit."[x] Only God the Father can meet the
longings of our children, as He does our own. The Father
does this in Christ through the Holy Spirit. How shall a
parent stay present to the child in a fallen world?

Staying Warmly Present by Embracing the Sorrow

How do children, then, experience God and the Gospel? One of the primary ways children experience the Gospel is by the non-anxious presence of the parents; that is, when parents remain warmly present in the midst of unmet longings and anxiety. Children experience the Gospel when parents offer presence – a non-anxious presence. The constant and trusting presence of a parent warmly present to offer grace is the first and best way for a child to find rest in Jesus Christ.

We are made in God's image – male and female. We were built for God and a better world. No parent or child is enough, nor is a spouse because only God can satisfy our deepest longings for deep relationship and love. Our longings tell us that we each have glory, that are made in God's image, and a day is coming when we shall all be fully satisfied in Him. Therefore, every parent will never be enough for their children, nor is any child enough for a parent. Longings for perfect love can only be met in God – the Father, the Son, and the Holy Spirit.

Whenever anxiety or anger is present it is a clear sign like a dashboard light on a car, which informs us that we must open up the hood of our heart and ask what is it that we long for that is unmet. Why is the dashboard on the surface of our lives showing signs of anxiety and anger? Our default mode is to demand that our longings be met, but in order to stay warmly present in human relationships we must embrace the sorrow of an unmet longings. In his novel *Redburn*, Herman Melville writes, "Not till we know, that one grief outweighs ten thousand joys, will we become what Christianity is striving to make us."[xi]

Sorrow and longings are legitimate, but anxiety and anger are not. Anxiety is the first sign that one's longing has become an idol or a demand. It may be a casual longing to be on time for school, a critical and relational longing to deeply connect with others, or a crucial longing for God to satisfy the soul. Staying warmly present requires us to embrace the sorrow and repent of unreasonable demands on other people we love most, which keeps anxiety and anger at bay.

Children want their parents to be involved in their lives. What I recall about little league baseball was my father's cheers when I hit well, and the way he sat with me in the car after games when I did not. My father took me to my first MLB game, which was a taste of heaven because we were together in a sea of thousands. When I think of baseball I think of my father. One boy came to his father with a cap, mitt, bat, and ball while his dad was busy on the computer again and said: "Dad, either play with me, or trade me." The problem is that no parent will ever be enough for a child, and the child will have to embrace the sorrow of unmet longings.

It is not possible, nor wise, for a parent to keep a child from sorrow. Embracing sorrow leads to healing and prayer for what no one but God can control. One of the reasons parents and children do not stay warmly present to each other is an unwillingness to embrace sorrow. If we don't, then we tend to deaden our longings. For a child to live in the presence of an anxious and angry parent is to raise the child in a state of misery. Parents who do not learn to embrace sorrow and teach their children will have to endure the dreadful environment of living with anxious and demanding children. Anger and contempt function to block sorrow, and keep us from staying warmly and honestly present to reality, God, and each other.

Embrace the sorrow of unmet longings, teach your children to live like the Man of sorrows, and their longings will remain alive and their souls will heal from life's pains. In this way our children will be less prone not to live for the applause of people, and more likely to have their longings set in motion by the groan for heaven and God. The tears of your children are your praises; their anxieties and fits of rage your shame. Keep a warm and non-anxious presence with your children by embracing the sorrow of unmet longings together, then you will be able to establish your child's sense of Gospel identity.

How to Establish Gospel Identity in Children

Identity begins by naming children, but there is much more to this. Parents without a clear sense of identity in Christ are unable to establish a clear sense of Gospel identity in their children. Paul David Tripp writes, "If you are not resting as a parent in your identity in Christ, you will look for identity in your children."[xii] Therefore, a good place to begin is by looking back at what our parents' messages were to us before we can see the importance of our own – the message of the Gospel.

The Generational Messages of Parents

What was your mother's message to you, if you could narrow it down to one sentence? What was your father's message to you? What was your family's message? Often these messages do not reflect the Gospel. They are usually rules for life like: "Work hard and be successful," or they are based on a lie like: "Your voice doesn't matter, so keep quiet and do what I tell you." Some relate to emotions like, "Emotions must be stuffed." Sometimes they are related to hiding family shame and keeping ridiculous secrets like, "Our family is ideal, so demonstrate loyalty at all times (even though it is dysfunctional)." Messages that fall short of the Gospel must be renounced because only the Gospel has the authority to rule us.

One way to think about your own message to your children is through the framework of three texts – the Gospel text, the child's context, and the subtext of your own heart. Gospel maturity of a parent is known by examining the parent's subtext. The subtext is the message under your message. It is the real, intended meaning (conscious or unconscious) of a message, which is deeper than the surface meanings of the words. Your tone of voice, facial expression, posture, and gestures will do a lot of work to signal your real message to your child, and that goal can hijack the communication process regardless of your clear Gospel statements.

One parental subtext is one of reinforcement: "We are the best family and here's why." Although it is good to give a sense of family unity and identity, it can hinder the Gospel's power to transform your children's lives. These parents create a pressure to conform to a tribal behavior and dialect that may not prepare children for adult years. Another parental subtext is one of performance. The message underneath the message is: "Don't you think we are great parents, and don't you think this is a super family? Don't you want to obey us, strive for success, and contribute to the family's image?" The performance goal is "Look at me; listen to me. See how worthy I am of your respect."

The problem here is that every parent desires to establish credibility with his or her children, but if this becomes the main goal, it disintegrates the parent's ability to speak the Gospel clearly in order to change their children's lives. Self-conscious parents draw attention to themselves, not to Christ. Children must not feel the parents are selling a message about themselves in a way that makes the Gospel unreal. We must not preach the Gospel as fiction and act out a fiction as truth.

Every parent has a subtext. If we are seeking to raise children into Gospel maturity, then our subtext matters. In giving our children the Gospel what we are really saying is: "Isn't Christ beautiful? Let us taste and see His goodness all our days." It is a message that aims beyond a lecture on God, the parents' expectations for good behavior, or correct knowledge of doctrine. It is more about how a child's affections become fixed upon Christ in awe and wonder through the parents' real message under their spoken message. Therefore, generational messages of parents must be taken captive and brought into line with the Gospel's message in order to establish a solid sense of identity in Christ.

The Interpretation War

Satan loves to keep believers under the rule of condemnation and lies. If he can get a foothold in our families then he can stimulate conflicts.[xiii] Every parent and child is vulnerable to a central condemning thought (CCT) or core lie, even a basic fear. That is why a personality test like the Enneagram can name nine personalities based on nine core fears or lies that we each live out of and develop autonomous and foolish strategies to form a personality. Most personality tests pinpoint a pathological approach to life that must be replaced by the Gospel.[xiv]

When Karen and I were trying to understand our five children we prayed to God that we would not lean on our own understanding but acknowledge Him in parenting (Proverbs 3:5-6). We wondered if each child was more like one of us by comparing them to ourselves, but when the children were all old enough we all took the Enneagram test only to discover we were all different. Karen was a six, I was a four, and the children and their spouses were nine, threes, a seven, an eight, a six, a one, and a four. Each was living out of a CCT or core lie that the evil one had given about our identities, and our default mode was to employ foolish strategies to overcome or prove that we were not the condemned kind of person that Satan accused us of.

Children, and parents, wrongly look to others to tell us who we are. Who have you given the authority to interpret your identity? Who do your children give the authority to tell them their true identity? Although parents play a significant role in giving a child an identity by naming them and speaking into their lives, the only one who has that ultimate authority is Christ. God tells us our gender, our name, and the truth of the Gospel. Parents are called to Gospel their children by uncovering the CCT that each parent and child feels is true, by asking whether it comes from God or the evil one, and by asking how their lies has functioned for them over the years.

Finding our Identity in Christ

In my book *Embracing Your True Identity in Christ: Renouncing Lies and Foolish Strategies*[xv] I show how each of us has a central condemning thought or core lie (CCT) that Satan has supplied to make sense out of our stories and our identity. Evil's answer to our identity is condemning. Mine is that I am unwanted as significant in community. My foolish strategies have been to redouble my efforts to prove that I am significant and special in community – family and work. No matter how hard we try to prove the CCT wrong, we eventually from time to time surrender to the lie. So we are forever swinging back and forth from trying to overcome it and surrendering to it as true. A parent's identity cannot come from performing as a parent, or to try to establish identity through the children. It comes by embracing one's identity in Christ, which frees up the parent to love the child and give the child a solid sense of identity in Christ as well.

A child's first question is a question that must be answered; namely, who am I? It is a Christian parent's essential task to give the child a solid identity in Christ. This starts with gender identity. It begins by delighting in a child's gender by affirming masculinity or femininity in the child. Of course, once the gender is revealed, the parents name the child with an honorable name that calls forth noble character and meaningful existence – a name that is also suitable to the child's gender. Names have meaning, but God already gives gender on the front end. Gender comes from outside of us. God gives it; it is who God says the child is. The parent affirms the child's identity and names the child with delight, and in this way the parents are giving the child the Gospel from the time of birth.

One of the most instructive ways a parent can give a child a solid sense of Identity in Christ is to announce the glory and the ruin of the child's gender so that the child can understand why he or she experiences both the glory and brokenness of gender in order to look for a redeemer in the Person of Christ. As an experienced pastor I have recognized that gender dysphoria or confusion has become a primary concern among parents. Gender dysphoria is the condition of feeling one's emotional and psychological identity as male or female to be opposite to one's biological sex.

Sons and Daughters are "Glorious Ruins"

God spoke very intentionally according to the original Hebrew in Genesis 1: 26– 28: "Let us make man in our image, male (zakar) and female (neqebah)." Parents of sons, God intended for your child to be a man and not a woman. Parents of daughters, God intended for her to be female and not male. God differentiated masculinity and femininity to be glorious, different, yet equal in glory.

God delights in girls and being female, just as He does for boys being masculine. One of our common struggles, however, is that we do not delight in who God made our children's gender in the same way He does. Children may struggle over why God made them male or female, and parents can greatly help children embrace their true identity.

Both sons and daughters need "vitamin F" from mothers and "vitamin M" from fathers. Mothers are the ones who, for the most part, are the primary caretakers of young children, and the "vitamin F" they offer is essential. It is summed up in one word; namely, *well-being*. Whereas fathers offer more active delight and an essential role in calling out each child to differentiate from their parents and siblings, mothers may recognize from an early age that issues of identity formation are different for boys than they are for girls.

Female identity formation takes place in the milieu of an ongoing relationship in which a daughter can identify herself as like her mother. Sons, on the other hand, recognize from early on that they must separate or differentiate from their mother if they are to define themselves as masculine. Their father, the person with whom they could identify strongly with as a male is usually less available to them. Thus, separation and individuation are critically tied to gender identity for sons; while for daughters, issues of feminine identity do not depend as much on the achievement of separation from the mother as much until teen years.[xvi]

In summary, parents spend most of the early years of childhood affirming the glory of their children's gender as sons and daughters, and to affirm the differences. Parents also, however, must acknowledge that being male and female is not only glorious but also fallen. C. S. Lewis calls people "glorious ruins" because we are made in God's image, but are also fallen in need of salvation. In the words given to the children of C. S. Lewis' *Narnia* series in *Prince Caspian*: "You come of the Lord Adam and the Lady Eve, and that's both honor enough to lift up the head of the poorest beggar, and shame enough to bow the shoulders of the greatest emperor on earth."[xvii]

The Glory and Ruin of Sons

What is so glorious about a son? God made men from the dust in Genesis chapter two, and boys love dirt and mud if you'll let them. Sons were built to work the dirt and cultivate it with a special relationship to the earth. Sons long to have an impact and be significant in their doings. Sons are built to provide fruit from it and to protect. They are natural army men as Adam was built to guard the tree of the knowledge of good and evil. They are glorious when they pursue a godly woman in older years, and are meant to leave their mother and father and pursue her like lady wisdom in Proverbs chapter eight. Sons are made like Adam to sing poetic love and delight of women and to leave.

It is the father's role, and mother's knowing, to call them out into greatness and pursuit of their bent – training them in the way they should go. For now, boys are fallen in their attempt to make a great impact on the world. Dr.

James Dobson shared confessions of men, who expressed their glory in fallen ways in their youth. For example, one man from the state of Washington (born in 1952) wrote:

> A friend and I found a coffee can of gasoline in the garage and decided to pour some down a manhole, light it, and see what would happen. We popped the manhole open, poured some gas in, and replaced the cover so that it was ajar. We kept throwing matches down but nothing happened, so we poured all the gas in. Finally, there was a noise like a jet engine starting up, and then a big BOOM! The manhole cover flew up and a flame shot up fifteen feet in the air. The ground was rumbling like an earthquake, and the manhole cover crashed about twelve feet away in the neighbor's driveway. What happened was the gas ran down the sewer lines for a block or so and vaporized with all the methane in there, and blew ups all our neighbors' toilets. I'm a plumber now; that's how I know exactly what happened.[xviii]

Ever since the fall, however, every son feels a deep sense of inadequacy in order to achieve greatness. The masculine curse was meant to help men come to an end of their efforts and cry out for redemption. Until they embrace their weakness they will never ask Christ to display His strength in and through them.

Adam was present but silent when Eve dialogued with Satan. He didn't protect her, then hid and blamed God and her for his failure. Learning to admit failure is key to receiving salvation and grace from another man; namely, Jesus Christ.

When a son receives God's covering of righteousness of his shame and pardon for his guilt, then he can be transformed by the Gospel to enter fully into his calling. Every son is a glorious ruin, but a glorious ruin redeemed is on his way to glory once more.

The Glory and Ruin of Daughters

In Genesis chapters two and three God reveals to us the glory and ruin of each gender. Daughters were made from the rib of Adam. Whereas sons may be clueless about relationships at first, daughters are relational. They are made from man and not the dust. Matthew Henry describes the first marriage and the glory of being female. He wrote: "The woman was made of a rib out of the side of Adam; not made out of his head to rule over him, nor out of his feet to be trampled upon by him, but out of his side to be equal with him, under his arm to be protected, and near his heart to be beloved."

Our twins were born after our first three children – a daughter and two sons. Our twins, Ethan and Lizzy, expressed great loyalty to each other, although Lizzy's very first sentence caused doubt. When the two of them were about two years old, they were gated into the living room. One time I came in and asked who pulled the books off the shelves, Lizzy replied with her first sentence ever: "Ethan did it." Ethan was the strong protector for Lizzy, and Lizzy helped Ethan about the dynamics of relationships at school together.

Daughters are glorious because of their relational nurturing, beauty, and strong support. Whereas sons leave for significance, daughters are given. They long for security more as sons long for significance. It is the parents' role to affirm that their daughter is enough as a woman to be pursued by a man like the godly and wise woman of Proverbs. A father not only affirms her beauty and gender but also promises to walk her into our Father's world and down an aisle to the right man so that she feels secure. A father affirms her gender as a woman like her mother but separate as a woman in her own right, which is crucial in teen years when mother and daughter tensions increase.

Daughters are not only glorious; they are ruins. Ever since Genesis chapter three women want to know more than they should know, hide their shame and blame-shift their guilt like men. The feminine curse means that every daughter feels she is too much, whereas every son feels he is not enough. Daughters, like women, are crouched to control their primary relationships. God, in His goodness, directed the masculine and feminine curse at each gender glory so that each would admit that they couldn't find significance or security without a redeemer. When a daughter admits she is insecure and that her foolish strategies to get her feminine longings met will never work by controlling others through beauty et al, then she will cry out for a Christ to save her as the hero

in her story – the one who will slay the dragon, pursue
her in marriage, and provide the security she always
longed for. When she finds her rest in Christ, then she is
on her way to glory.

Warfare: Fighting for your child

Parenting, then, is an invitation given to our children to
look to God as three persons in the one true God, even as
they look to parents to demonstrate an unshakable bond of
love by keeping their covenant vows in marriage.
Children must look to our Heavenly Father as the father
they always longed for, who made them male and female.
His voice is heard in the words, "You are My son or
daughter in whom I am well pleased." It is an invitation to
admit that the gender curses were intended for them to
confess that they are licked without a Redeemer and that
they would cry out to Christ for redemption and worth.
This leads to an experience of the Holy Spirit poured out
upon their thirsty souls in order that these children of
promise may become *like willows by flowing streams of
water.*

Because children were made in the image of God they
long for so much more than this life offers. Learning to
live with unmet longings and to *embrace the sorrow* of
their longings - a son wanting significance and a daughter
longing for security – will keep them from anxiety and
anger. It will keep your family *warmly present* to one
another.

Evil's assaults are aimed at the vulnerable, which means
children. Children need a Gospel interpretation about their

identity and who they are, which comes mainly through their parents. Because children tend to believe Satan's lie and CCT, children need parents to encourage them to renounce Satan's lie and condemning thought. When Satan attacks, he doesn't leave his fang bites on your neck and physical scars on your face. Rather, he leaves a poisonous lie in your heart that must be taken out as soon as possible.[xix] They need Parental help to recognize their foolish strategies as unproductive, and may lead to surrender to the lie and discouragement from time to time. Parents must be engaged in warfare against evil with the weapons of love and truth. Too many parents speak truth as fiction, but live fiction as truth.

Finally, parents must fight against culture's confusion about gender, and return to the bible's teaching about the glory and ruin of masculinity and femininity so that they cry out for God to redeem them as sons and daughters on their way to glory.

In the next chapter we will consider children as a gift from God, which engenders parental gratitude to the Lord. It will invite parents to embrace God's promise and vision for their children in His story and world, and call forth faith in God's faithfulness to His promises for their children.

Discussion Questions

1. What does it mean to stay warmly present to your spouse and children?

2. Why is it necessary to help children embrace the sorrow of unmet longings?

3. What was your father's message to you as a child? What was your mother's message to you? How do these relate to the message of the Gospel of God?

4. What is the glory of being masculine? How does every boy or man struggle with a sense of inadequacy since the masculine curse in Genesis 3? How does your son find grace when he admits he is licked without strength from Christ? What does a redeemed man look like?

5. What is the glory of being feminine? How can you affirm this in your daughter? How does every girl or woman struggle with a sense of loneliness since the feminine curse in Genesis 3? How does a woman's heart feel too much, and try to control her primary relationships? What does a redeemed woman look like?

Chapter Two: Children of Promise

This chapter, "Children of Promise," explains the implications of what it means that children are not only gifts from God but also come with the promise of God. Parenting begins with giving thanks and offering our children back to God in faith. Even as we name our children, we are calling out our children to live as God's gifts to the world, trusting God to author their story of promise.

Unless the LORD builds the house,
   those who build it labor in vain.
Unless the LORD watches over the city,
   the watchman stays awake in vain.
It is in vain that you rise up early
   and go late to rest,
eating the bread of anxious toil;
   for he gives to his beloved sleep.
Behold, children are a heritage from the LORD,
   the fruit of the womb a reward.
Like arrows in the hand of a warrior
   are the children of one's youth.
Blessed is the man
   who fills his quiver with them!
He shall not be put to shame
   when he speaks with his enemies in the gate.   Psalm 127

Children are a Gift from the Lord

Children are gifts from God, given for parents to enjoy God more fully. God is building your home, "the house," with you. Unless God was the builder, you could have the home or any children. Children are meant to fuel gratitude. Although parents "go late to rest" and "rise up early" to care for their children, it does not have to be in vain when thankfulness keeps you going. Parenting is one of the most meaningful callings in our service to God on behalf of others.

Mothers who stay home from working outside the home to nurture their little one may feel less significant at times when day after day it demands every ounce of energy to see a child reach the one-year birthday. She is recovering a birthing process that required all her body's effort. There is no salary, little affirmation, and discouragement mixed with exhaustion is a common experience. All year that mother is reminded of two truths; her child is a gift from God and a child of promise. Regarding her past she raises her Ebenezer by which she means, "Thus far the Lord has been my help;" and concerning the future she trusts Jehovah-Jira, believing "the Lord will provide."

It is in this first season of parenting that parents need the Gospel and constant reminders that God has been good to them in the past and will be in the future by giving them a very personal gift – a child of promise.

Gratitude to God for Your Children

Giving thanks to God is the first and primary way to fuel parents with the energy they will need to not only nurture their little one, but also to gratefully accept the child God gave them. In some cases God's gift is a special needs child, which is usually an unexpected surprise to parents.

As a pastor in a growing church of young married couples desiring healthy children, I have come alongside a good number of parents grieving their first weeks as parents over the discovery that their child has been diagnosed with a syndrome of one sort or another. For example, we have children born with Down Syndrome and Turner Syndrome. We have cried out to the Lord with friends and family for healing as the parents went from rejection and shock, to tolerance and finally to acceptance of God's will for them to pick up their cross and walk into the future they had not anticipated. In every case, however, they have been motivated by this one truth that their child is a gift from God. Besides, these children become adults in who we have pure delight. They teach us gratitude, faith, and what it means to love well.

One of the ways these parents will testify to God's grace is that they confess that their child drew them much closer to the Lord as they embraced being their little one's advocate for life. Special needs children are special gifts children, for grace is made manifest in weakness. Our congregation joins in with these parents with a deeper appreciation and love for God and these little ones. There isn't a Sunday morning at church that goes by that I do not receive a hug and a smile from a special needs adult child. They often show me a Special Olympics medal they one, and we talk about movies they enjoy. Children are a gift from the Lord, and these parents and children are very valuable to us because they are under the Chief Shepherd's eye; namely, Christ's heart.

Many of our church's families are so grateful for special needs children that the parents compassionately and intentionally seek such children out from all over the world to adopt them into their families. This remarkable sight and experience is evidence that the world will know we are Christians by our love.

Family life draws us to pleasure in God. Fathers and mothers, and their children, are pointing us to the enjoyment of God. Jonathan Edwards shared how this is true when he wrote:

> To go to heaven, fully to enjoy God, is infinitely better than the most pleasant accommodations here. Better than fathers and mothers, husbands, wives, or children . . . These are but shadows; but the enjoyment of God is the substance.

Children are a gift from the Lord. Blessed are the parents whose quiver is full of them and filled with gratitude welling up to God, for family life is meant to draw us upward to the full enjoyment of God in Heaven.

Naming Children for God's Glory and Story

Family names tell the family's story in God's providence, often in relation to the narrative of redemptive history. For example, Abraham means "father of many." Isaac, born to his parents in their old age, means "laughter." Their names and lives tell identity stories, and all their stories are connected to the gospel story and narrative at large— God's providence is recorded in the historically reliable acts of God's redemptive work throughout the generations of humanity with settings, characters, and a plot. The plot is a purposeful arrangement of events with a beginning, middle, and end. The child's plot in God's story has tension leading to resolution in Jesus Christ as his or her Savior and Lord. The Bible unfolds its' narrative from innocence to fall, and from redemption to consummation.

Providence is the gift your heart was made to want, which gave you a sense of being authored and enjoying the Author's perspective (an authority to trust while interpreting its meaningful plot). Plot elevates chronos (time as we know it) to the felt level of kairos (God's story time). Your story is God's story, and the tension of His plot is felt in the suffering, longings, and struggling for God to resolve them.

What is your heart's quest, which your inner self longs to surmount but requires you to trust God for? How does evil tempt you to escape the tension of waiting on God in faith? God gave you a story with a plot, an evil enemy, and a happy consummation to envision overcoming all obstacles. However ordinary your life's story may appear, I believe you will know within that it has transcendence and a deeper meaning for a larger story with eternal consequences.

Your Child's Story

Before you gave your child a name, your child was. Psalm 139:15– 16 honors God as the author of our individual story by mentioning our lives were written in His "book."

He, who knew your child before he or she was made, knew and knitted your child together before she or he was born in her mother's womb. For your child to know her story is for her to know how God will shape her into a new creation in Christ with a past, a present, and a future. Her story has a redemptive plot. The tension of this plot weaves themes until it is resolved through owning her true identity in Christ, fulfilling her God-given destiny, and overcoming regret and busyness with intentionality, until a glorious resolution of grace prevails from her Gospel legacy.

Believers are leaving a Gospel blessing with one arm stretched out over the next generation and another reaching for the upward prize as you are crossing the river of death when they will receive the festal shout of heaven's welcome. Your child's life story, and a clear identity in Christ, is what matters most when it comes to God's story.

Your Child's Name

When we name our children we are stewarding God's gift. Parents are given stewardship of their children to raise them and send them off into their callings. They do not own their children; God does. Christian names are outward expressions of what people are inwardly good at being, doing, and demonstrating. When Adam named the first woman Eve (Life-giver), he had the power to peer into her glory and to draw out her calling. To this day, a spouse's and a parent's voice trumps all other voices with the authority to enhance or to degrade. Jesus perceived Simon (Pebble) had a greater heart and glory than his outward name expressed. So Jesus renamed him Peter (Rock).

What is your child's given name, his or her full name, and why was he or she given that name? What does his first, last, and middle names literally express by way of family meaning? For example, parents often name children after another family relative or a culturally and biblically important person. Whatever your child's name is, it will shape him in some way.

Who had authority to name Jesus? His parents did not, because God the Father told Joseph to name his son Jesus to express that His glory was like the name Joshua (renamed by Moses from Hosea), which meant He will save His people. Jesus is not stewarded. He only names others, us. He has named each Christian with a new name written in heaven, which was meant to shape us on our journey to discover our destiny.

Dedicating Your Children to God

Lose your children for Jesus' sake and you will keep them. Try to keep and control your children, and you'll lose them. In the bible children were given the sign of God's covenant of promise as babies at eight days old in the Old Testament through circumcision of males. In the New Testament the sign and seal of the covenant of grace is baptism, which includes both male and female babies of at least one believing parent because they are holy in some sense. They are holy to the Lord (1 Cor. 7:14). The promise that God will pour out His Spirit upon them like

water on their thirsty souls comes to them before they
even sought God at all.

Whether in baptism or in dedication, the pastor blesses the
child. For example, if it is a boy, the pastor might say in
faith:

> You are a son of promise. The promise of the
> Father is to your parents and to you, and to your
> children's children to another 1,000 generations.
> May God our Father, who has had it on His heart
> from all eternity to glorify His Son, pour out the
> Spirit of adoption and make you cry out: "Abba!
> Father!"   back   to   Him.
>
> May He Unite you to Christ – regenerate,
> effectually call, and assure you that you are His
> and He is yours. The Lord cleanse you from sin,
> mortify it, and raise you from it to new life at an
> early age, for Jesus has said: "For such children
> like   you   belongs   the   kingdom."
>
> Since you are received into His visible church and
> bound to renounce and fight the world, the flesh,
> and the devil, may you become strong in your
> weakness to serve as an officer in His church –
> mighty in the scriptures and God's friend in
> prayer like Jacob who wrestled with God until he
> was   given   a   new   name.
>
> The Lord give you a godly wife, godly children,

godly children in law, godly grandchildren until our Lord comes again in glory.
Amen

This dedication of your child to God on the front end teaches us that however much a separation will come when parents are empty-nesters, sons and daughters are not for parents to vicariously live their lives through. Children must never rule a parent's life as functional idols in your heart. To this end God has given parents His precious and very great promises.

God is Faithful to His Promises

Isaiah 44:3-5 begins with a command to parents to not live by fear, but to look to God by faith in this promise for their children, which reads:

> For I will pour water on the thirsty land and streams on the dry ground; I will pour My Spirit upon your offspring, and My blessing on your descendants. They shall spring up among the *grass like willows by flowing streams*. This one will say, "I am the Lord's," and another will call on the name of Jacob, and another will write on his hand, "The Lord's," and name himself by the name of Israel.

God calls forth faith from parents to trust His promise to be faithful to their children, who were not born by chance to believing parents but by His divine will. Parents must not be ruled by fear and anxiety but by faith in God's vision for their future; God is trustworthy. Fear makes parents vulnerable and discouraged when they hear the many stories of how Christian children have not grown up to become godly believers. When trials come and teenage children make evident that they are not born again our faith is tested and our greatest fear increases, but we must go back to God's promises in His word and cry out in faith for their salvation through the outpouring of the Holy Spirit.

Karen and I invested our lives and the Gospel into our children. I remember taking out a picture of my family at a large men's conference among 60,000 men being challenged to turn my heart towards home. I stared at our family picture and wept as I sensed God's call to become a father who invests in our little rascals. We trained them in the word, theology, calling, sex, work, and all areas of life. They knew the Gospel and heard me preach the Gospel each Sunday. Karen and I prayer over the promises of God that they would be born again, but when they became teen-agers it became evident that three of the five were not yet saved.

The Free Gift of Salvation

One week our third oldest, Jonathan, was grounded. At the end of the week when I came home after work Karen said that he was unrepentant. "Jonny," I said, "what's going on?" Jonny said with tear-filled eyes, "I don't know. I sing God's praise and know the Gospel, but my heart isn't in it." I replied, "Maybe you are not saved. It is okay to admit it." He paced back and forth in the kitchen before the loving eyes of his mother and father like the loving eyes of the trinity. He tossed his cell phone on the table and said he was going for a ride. He left in the car, and Karen looked to me to lead and perhaps stop him. I said, "Let us let him go, but pray." We sought the Lord for the outpouring of the Holy Spirit on our knees. After about an hour he come home with puffy eyes. Our family liked to play a basketball game called "knockout," and we all just shot baskets for a while in the driveway – all seven of us. I said, "Jonny, what's up? Would you like to talk?" We all went into the living room and plopped on the sofa.

Jonathan shared what happened. He had driven far out into the country to a gravel road, got out of the car, and laid prostrate on the road crying out to the Lord for the Holy Spirit until he was assured of salvation. Then he directed his attention to his younger brother and sister (the twins), and said that although he was saved he wasn't sure if they were. As he asked penetrating questions, Lizzy said she was, but Ethan kept slouching lower in the sofa and cam to sit right next to Jonathan. As he spoke of his experience, Ethan confessed he wasn't saved and that he wanted to be. I encouraged him to settle it right there, but that we were not going to tell him how to pray. "Just cry out to the Lord," I said. "Whoever cries out to the Lord shall be saved." We got on our knees, Ethan cried out to the Lord, we all wept, and God gave him a new heart.

Ethan went right to the phone, called his dearest friends, and said: "I just became a Christian!" They said, "We thought you were already a Christian." Ethan said, "No, but I am now." That was one of the happiest days of our lives. Another day was yet to come, however, for our oldest daughter was still to try our faith.

Our daughter Emily began to drift away from the Lord in college a few years later. The more we heard from her or others, the more our hearts broke. Eventually, mother's day became a crisis. As we confronted her and she came to realize that maybe she was not yet saved, she went off radar for a week. I was the only one she texted, and Karen and I were back in the labor room for our daughter – the labor room of prayer. I literally crawled on our kitchen floor begging God for her soul. I wept over Isaiah 44:2-3 with my finger on the page, asking God for her salvation.

By the week's end we met briefly for Mother's Day, and then a few days later she came to a guy's home that I was training in discipleship. She stayed alone in a private room reading the bible when he heard her throw the bible against the wall. He shared with her the doctrine of justification from Romans chapter five, and Emily repented and put her faith in Christ. Suddenly Karen and I received a text: "Can we meet as a family?" We texted back: "Yes!"

Emily came home and we all sat down on the sofa to listen. She began to share in tears her new heart for a new life with Christ. Her cell phone was ringing, but she kicked it away. She determined that nothing was going to get in her way of Christ from then on. She shared how she found peace with God and was justified in Christ – pardoned of all her sins and accepted as righteous in His sight by faith alone. We all rejoiced, played a softball game, and a week later in a college prayer meeting she received a tremendous filling of the Holy Spirit. That was one of the best days of our lives as parents. Soon a godly man, Tyson, courted her. They married, had four children, and Emily became a pastor's wife thriving in a ministry context. I'll never forget the day of Emily's birth when joy and tears flowed as I dedicated her up in the air to Almighty God, and the day He truly took hold of her for His own glory.

God is faithful to His promises for the children of believing parents, but trusting God and not being ruled by circumstances and disappointments requires parents to trust God through the labor pains of a second birth like that of a mother giving birth to her child on the day of birth. God gave Karen and me five gifts and ten birthing labors, and we are so grateful for each of them. We named them, knowing they each have a story written by the Author of life. Their stories were not written the way we would have written them. We gave each of our children biblical and family names, meaningful names, and dedicated them to God as babies. As parents we have had our faith tested and refined by fire until it became more precious than gold. This kind of faith in God's promises will give you, as a parent, the proper posture for parenting; one of gratitude and faith. The next chapter describes the kind of posture a parent will take before their children and God.

Discussion Questions

1. How have you become grateful for your children?

2. What are your children's names? What do their names mean? Why did you name them accordingly?

3. How might your children's names relate to the story God is written for them and is slowly revealing through Hiss providence?

4. When did you dedicate your child to God? Why was that meaningful to you?

5. Your child is a child of promise. What does it mean to trust God's promise in Isaiah 44:2-5 without fear? How is that going?

6. How have you offered the free gift of salvation to your children? How have you helped your child be honest about whether or not he or she is truly saved?

Chapter Three: The Posture of Parenting

In some sense children raise parents because God brings parents down to their knees, quieted like a weaned child silent before God, renewed to a position of Gospel repentance, and learning to the school of wisdom.

Parents are Given to Children by God

The first posture a parent takes is that of being given by God as a gift to children. Matthew begins with: "The book of the genealogy of Jesus Christ, the son of David, the son of Abraham . . . Joseph the husband of Mary, of whom Jesus was born, who is called Christ" (Matthew 1:1,17). Jesus was given a heritage, a family, and a set of parents, and through Jesus the path was opened for His parents to know themselves and God. We grow in our knowledge of God and ourselves through our relationship with our children, who are dependent on our care for them.

We don't choose our parents, and therefore our names and identity are given to us. Our identity isn't a matter of merit but of grace, and grace is hard to accept and impossible to resist. Whatever challenges I had with embracing the identity God gave me, I found that part of that struggle was accepting the parents He gave me. Now I laugh at my struggles to embrace them and myself, and realize my love for them as my dear parents. Indeed, I miss them terribly.

I wish I could have known my mother when she was a child and a young mother. I recently pulled out of an old box a picture of her as a little, adorable girl. The more I understand her story, the more compassion and understanding I have for her. Her father died when she was twelve years old. Poverty threatened to take away her privileges, but she remarkably won a scholarship to Lake Forrest College near Chicago where she met my father after his WWII service in the Navy.

My father grew up nearby in Winnetka, Illinois. His father was a pastor's son in Vermont. He was a gift of God to his six children. My friends told me in childhood that they wished he was their father. Whenever I expressed my appreciation for my father he would say with a smile, "My father was better than yours." He taught me to see parents as a gift from God. I come from a long line of fathers, many of them were pastors, who were marked by gentleness and kindness – a characteristic I admire and trust will continue through my sons.

Another photo caught my attention. It is a romantic photo (funny, too, for my Dad was always humoring her) when my parents were engaged. They had six children, I was the last one in the litter. They loved each other until the end of their lives on earth. I was privileged to lead them to faith in Christ during their final years of life when I was only in my thirties. As I preached and officiated their funerals, which were my first two funerals of many as a pastor, I realized that parents are given by God as gifts to their children.

Have you ever gazed at your parents' old pictures in a way that forced you to embrace who *you* are? Who *they* are? It is a *process* during adulthood where *points* in time become clarifying moments about one's true and God-given identity. Parents who see themselves as God's gifts to their children should not promote arrogance, but humility for the privilege of parenting.

Jesus accepted His identity not only as the Christ but also as a Jew in a long line of the good, bad, and the ugly. He did this to communicate His willingness to include and accept the greatest and the least into His family. The first posture a parent takes is that of a gift given by God to one's children. Pause and consider that you are God's gift to your child until you are humbled by its' prospect.

Children bring Parents to their Knees

Children raise parents into Gospel maturity by bring parents to their knees, to the cradle, to wait patiently for their children to grow into Gospel maturity. The first pose of parenting is the posture of dependency – the posture of a child of God depending on Him for sustaining and granting biological life in general and the spiritual life in particular.

Each morning Karen and I go to our "prayer closets" our "war rooms." We are a holler away from each other, and I know what she is praying because it is what I am praying; namely the promises of God for each child, sons and daughters in law included, and grandchildren.

Our children brought us down to our knees before our Father in Heaven, and taught us to pray for the wisdom and knowledge of what it means to be a child of God. Our children brought us to our knees in the house of laughter and in the house of morning, but it is better to go to the house of mourning than to the house of laughter as Solomon says.

One morning I received a call from our oldest son Nate. "Ella died," he said. I immediately hit the floor of the kitchen when I discovered that our two-month-old granddaughter went home to be with the Lord, but my heart broke for Nate and his wife, Leigh Ann, in a heavy and traumatic way. Children bring parents to their knees. They had two older daughters, but their third couldn't make it through her illness. That was the hardest funeral I ever preached to a packed chapel full at Covenant Theological Seminary where Nate was in his final year. Filling one of the front rows of the chapel was a row of mothers who had lost a child along the way; comforting those with the comfort they had received in their worst moment of parenting.

It was also a moment where I wept with the greatest respect for my son, who taught me what it means to be a father full of courage and faith. The funeral ended with Nate and Leigh Ann leading us outside to sing together "How Great Thou Art." Watching him carry Ella's body in a little casket out in front of the throng of procession was a moment of glory and wisdom. How can I ever forget that moment! Nate and Leigh Ann, as grieving parents, displayed courage, faith, and love aimed at glorifying God in the face of our enemy – death. Children call their parents to trust our God of the resurrection, and to courageously walk into His future grace with a wound too deep for words.

Children bring us to our knees in faith that God is God, and we are His children raising children of promise into Gospel maturity. I saw that God fulfilled His promise; namely, that our son Nate became a *willow by flowing streams of living water*, and the dry ground and thirsty land was drenched with the outpouring of the Holy Spirit that day. Children bring parents down to their knees.

Children Bring Parents to Silence before God

Fifteen minutes of silence under God's smile is one of the most necessary and most difficult spiritual disciplines in the modern world for believers, let alone believing parents. What does it mean to be quiet and at rest under God's smile over us? One of our favorite things to do as parents was to go to each room and bed at night and gaze with a smile of delight over our children as they slept with their favorite blankets and cuddly, stuffed animals.

Silence before God, under His loving smile, for fifteen minutes each day followed by Psalm 131 will save you from living out of anxiety and impatience with people in your place of calling. The psalmist says:

> O Lord, my heart is not lifted up;
> My eyes are not raised too high;
> I do not occupy myself with things
> Too great and marvelous for me.
> But I have calmed and quieted my soul,

> Like a weaned child with its mother;
> Like a weaned child is my soul within me.

Children teach us to be silent before God like a weaned, satisfied child with our mother and answer the question, how has God taken care of us as His beloved children?

Parenting can be overwhelming. Thoughts too great for us swirl in the minds of parents in each new season of their children's lives. Parental anxieties become questions. Will my child behave and make godly friends in school? Will our children drive safely on the road? Will my child learn to control anger and tongue? How can we pay for the children's education? Who will they marry? Such questions are too big for us, and only God can answer them. If parents live out of anxiety and fear, they will parent accordingly. If, however, parents quiet their hearts in silence before God, they will discover the contentment of being like a weaned child before its' mother; silent and trusting without fear or anxiety. Effective parenting is about posture before God; it is a matter of being quieted in the depths of the soul without questions too great for parents to answer.

Children bring us to Repentance

God is like a father who had two sons. One was filled with longing and self-hatred. He ran away, but came home willing to be a slave. The Father, however, ran to the son and kissed him before he could give his rehearsed speech of how unworthy he has been as a son. The father turned around and ordered a feast to honor this son's homecoming. "My son was lost but now is found!"

Repentance for this son required him to get off from the dirt of self-hatred over his sin and to receive His father's grace, to sit at the center of the family table, and to become the person of honor for the family. Does that describe you? Are you the child that confesses your sins, but finds it hard to receive pardon and love in spite of your disobedience to the father?

The father goes out to the older brother and begs him to come celebrate his brother's return. The second son, however, expresses self-righteousness. "I have been such a good son, and you never threw a party for me?" This son is filled with entitlement and religion, not the Gospel.

Religion functions in three ways. First, it does things for God in order to put God in debt to him. Second, religion functions to separate the "good" people from the "bad" people. Third, religion always exalts you as superior over others. "I thank you, God, I am not like that sinner over there." This son learns to repent of religion and believe the Gospel. Does the older brother describe you? Are you putting before God your parenting righteousness in a way that demands God to reward you? Do you find it difficult to rejoice when other children convert and receive favor? Is your parenting marked by religion or the Gospel?

Jesus' parable in Luke's gospel, chapter fifteen, teaches parents as children of God that only Jesus was the ideal older brother, who lived a righteous life. He went after younger, disobedient brothers and brought them home. It calls for repentance of the worst of sins; namely, self-righteousness and religion. Parenting is a constant posture of repentance. Parents regularly fail to parent well, and must always return to their heavenly Father for sustaining a clear sense of sonship and love. Parents often serve God on behalf in remarkable ways, which easily tempts them to demand God for favor based on the merits of parenting. Therefore, parenting requires a regular renouncing of basing their favor with God on the foundations of self-righteousness.

Children tend to be one of these two children, either an unrighteous child who is feeling condemned or self-righteous child who is embracing a level of entitlement. To the degree that parents can discern both errors in their children and their own lives, both kinds of children can be invited to taste and see the sweetness of the Gospel.
Children not only shape parents posture of being God's gift to their children, of being brought down to their knees before God, of regularly turning back to God in repentance, but also of going off to the school of wisdom.

Children bring Parents to the School of Wisdom

Formulas won't work for parents, and those who think they do are foolish. Wisdom literature of the bible teaches parental truisms (Proverbs) and the absurdity of chasing after perfection in parenting (Ecclesiastes).

What we knew about parenthood before we had children was about a page long. The old adage tells of a parent that began with five theories for raising children, but after later the parent confesses: "Now I have five children and no more theories." Teen-age children do not think parents are all that wise anyway. Mark Twain quipped: "When I was a teen I thought my dad was so unwise, but five years later I was amazed at how wise he had become in such a short time." Children bring us to the school of wisdom. Since having children we have had to turn to Proverbs for God's wisdom. Chapters 1-9 teach parents that wisdom begins with a reverent knowledge of God and a humble knowledge of where a parent's wisdom ends and where God's wisdom begins.

In these opening chapters we read ten fatherly lessons to a child and four poems from "Lady Wisdom." In a way we hear from a wise father and mother. We learn to get wisdom and prize it above all else (Proverbs 4:7-8). The father tells us to cultivate reverent knowledge of God, to put on virtue, integrity, generosity, humility and more in order to experience success and peace rather than the misery of folly and shame – even ruin. Wisdom, personified as a woman, tells us that she is woven into the fabric of the universe. She is like a town crier, calling out from the center of town to become generous, to exercise justice, to avoid gossip and sexual immorality. In this way, God's way, we apply wisdom and become skillful parents in the school of wisdom; the school our children send us in order to become wise.

What follows in chapters 10-29 are hundreds of proverbs on gender relations, marriage, parenting, debt, alcohol, depression, anxiety, economics, speech, friendships, work, poverty, and godly character filtered through God's wisdom. The book ends with chapter 30, where the non-Israelite king, Agur, confesses he lacks wisdom until he turns to the scriptures that can make one wise unto salvation. Then he shares what his mother taught him from creation – the ant, the badger, the locust, and the spider. Lemuel, a non-Israelite king, wrote chapter 31. Lemuel writes a poem using an acrostic from the Hebrew alphabet of his mother – a noble woman, who applied God's wisdom to family, work, and community. Proverbs is a school of wisdom for parents.

Most of our evening walks together as parents were spent discussing each of our five children, now ten, with fourteen grandchildren. Each of our children was a separate case and challenge, which required us to lean not on our own understanding but on the Lord for wisdom to *raise them into Gospel maturity*. In fact, they were constantly changing and facing new challenges at each stage of life. Reward charts with stickers for chores completed didn't work past early childhood. Their chores were different, and so were the expectations for their behavior too. Each season was so new for us as parents that we were like children, learning in God's school of wisdom on how to *raise them into Gospel maturity*.

Children raise parents. They force us to see ourselves as God's instrumental gift to our children, they bring us down to our knees in dependent prayer like a child, they silence our fears and anxieties until we become like a weaned child before its mother, they regularly turn us to God in repentance from unrighteousness and self-righteousness, and they send us off to the school of wisdom.

The next chapter is also about wisdom; how to use the moments of discipline as an awesome opportunity to pour wisdom into children.

Discussion Questions

1. How have your children raised you in the Lord to become more mature?

2. How have your children brought you to your knees in prayer?

3. How have your children brought you to a point of silence before God like a weaned child with its' mother?

4. How have your children exposed your self-righteousness and unrighteousness in a way that you have become convinced that your only righteousness is Christ? How have you repented over the years, and come more fully to rest in faith in the Gospel?

5. How have you grown in wisdom as a parent where you more fully have gained wisdom from above in order to parent well?

Chapter Four: Gospel Discipline

One of the "musts" of raising children with folly bound up in their hearts is consistent, loving discipline – something both parents and children may be uncomfortable with experiencing. How shall parents discipline their children in love and why? This chapter sheds biblical light on the nature and purpose of discipline by reflecting on the two primary questions children are asking their parents, right and wrong ways to practice discipline, different forms of discipline, the three weightiest matters of discipline, and practical ways love must abound when it comes to discipline.

The Two Primary Questions Children Ask their Parents

Children are asking two basic questions when they a young.[xx] The first is: do you love me? The second is: can I have my way? The answer to the first question is always yes, but the second answer is often answered in the negative until a child learns wisdom and limitations. A parent's communication of love for their children implies both mercy and strength. God loves His children with tender mercy and kindness, but He does not let us have our way much of the time because He is wise and we are not. God disciplines us to live joyfully and with a freedom that makes our choices wiser and more in line with His. This He does with loving strength so that our wills are surrendered to His will for our good.

A parent who communicates that a child can have her way, while not showing love, is a dangerous parent. The child has to learn boundaries and rules because God and community living require them for peaceful relations. Parents who says how much they love their child, yet allows the child to have her way, raises the child without strength. Indulging in the child doesn't prepare her for life's limits and boundaries. This requires the parent to exercise strength of will over the child's choices that may lead her down a painful path.

A parent who answers both questions in the negative communicates rules without love; strength without tenderness and mercy. That is to say, children who do not feel love from parents and cannot have their way experience life without delight and only duty. This combination of little love and too much strength works together to answer a child's two basic questions in a way that leaves the child unmotivated to keep the rules. Tender loving-kindness and delight become the necessary inspiration for a family context that has high standards of behavior.

The reason for this is based on two assumptions about children. Children were built to long for validation of their glory. Everyone longs for never-failing love. Children are not wise enough, however, to know what is best for them. Their parents usually do. There are two proverbs that speak to our children's condition and need for strength from their parents. The first is Proverb 14:12, which reads: "There is a way that seems right to a man, but it is the way of death." The second teaches parents that children are born with folly bound up in their hearts, and that strong discipline will replace folly with God's wisdom. Proverb 22:15 states this truism: "Folly is bound up in the heart of a child. The rod of discipline will remove it far from them."

Therefore, parental strength combined with tender delight is a necessary and primary way to answer the two core questions children are asking their parents. When parents discipline their children they are answering the two questions; namely, "Yes, I love you and, no, you can't always have your way." Children are not only asking two basic questions, they often develop foolish approaches to their parents to get what they want from them. What are some of these foolish strategies that parents should recognize?

Three Ways Children Approach Parents Wrongly[xxi]

All of us are bent on folly. We are determined to live life autonomously without divine intervention, which parents armed with the Gospel can address. We are depraved, and our autonomous strategies attempt to meet the dignity of our longings without depending on God for grace through Jesus Christ.

Three of the ways this shows up is in the way children move towards, against, and away from their parents. Below are three generalizations of how folly is bound up in children, who would otherwise seem quite fine to parents unconcerned to raise their children into Gospel maturity. The Compliant Child, the Aggressive Child, and the Perfectionist Child need Gospel wisdom, which comes through loving discipline from Christian parents.

The Compliant Child

A compliant child is looking for affection and approval, anyone who will rescue him or her from what is perceived as the greatest need. This child moves *towards* parents. This category is seen as a process self-effacement and a false humility. A compliant child will use this strategy for facing fears related to the parents. It becomes evident when the child senses fear of powerlessness and abandonment.

Children within the compliance category tend to exhibit a need for affection and approval on the part of their parents, but may be prone to not owning the heart God gave them. They may also seek out a partner, somebody to confide in, fostering the belief that, in turn, the new cohort would relieve them of loneliness. This child appears humble because of his or her lack of demands on others combined with a desire to hide his or her need for grace and courage to differentiate from others. This child is likely to enmesh with a parent unwilling to call the child out into God's world to fulfill a unique calling and express one's glory. His or her message is "I am going to be good; just don't leave me."

On the one hand, the compliant child wants to keep a good and safe relationship with the parent. On the other hand, there is the great need for separation and differentiation from the parent(s) to bond with his or Father in heaven through Jesus Christ. This child remains bent-over towards the parent(s), and no parent will ever be enough for the cry of his or her soul. The father's role is to point them to God the Father as the Father the child always longed for, and to hear the words: "You are My son or daughter in whom I am well-pleased." The father is called to separate the child from the mother and call the child out and into the world.

A daughter needs to be affirmed by the father as a woman in her own right, like her mother in gender but different. She needs the security from her father that this is another Father's world, and that He has a safe place for her to fulfill her calling. The father can assure her that he will walk her out of the home, towards a school and vocation, and down an aisle for marriage. Daughters are given.

A son also needs a father to affirm his gender as a man, like his father but separate from mom and dad. The father must call out the son from a bent-over posture to a vertical one and to hear from God the Father: "You are My son in whom I am well-pleased." The parent(s) must channel him towards the pursuit of his calling and to pursue others for their welfare, even a godly woman for marriage and family. Whereas daughters are given, sons leave.

The compliant child must unite to Christ and come to terms with separation and differentiation in Christ, separating from being bent over towards his or her parents for the validation only God can give. The child must come to see that all his or her compliant righteousness is as filthy rags. Self-righteousness must be exposed as insufficient to win what he or she longs for in order to receive the free righteousness of Christ that Christ lived out for us. The compliant child may grow to love how Christ took all our unrighteousness and self-righteousness on Himself upon the cross to set us free from compliant strategies towards parents and others.

The Aggressive Child

A second category is the aggressive child, who longs for a sense of significance and power. This child moves *against* the parents. He or she may possess the ability to bend the wills of others in order to achieve control. This child is bent on exploiting others for prestige and social recognition. He or she desires personal admiration, and may become desperate for personal achievement. His or her message is "don't get in my way."

On the one hand, the aggressive child is an achiever and will perform well in life, which often pleases the parents. On the other hand, however, this child is bent over to get through performance in activities what only God can give; namely, validation and admiration. As the father affirms him or her in gender and calling, the parents also must expose how the child is self-centered and controlling in his or her strategies. This child must find rest in the Gospel in a way that leads to peace in his or her relationship with parents and any primary relationships. Until the aggressive child is turned from a bent-over posture to a vertical one by receiving validation and admiration from the Father through Jesus Christ, the child will remain seeking an independent strategy that hasn't learned what it means to rest in Christ's performance on his or her behalf so that the child will love others well without envy and competition to be superior over others.

The Perfectionist Child

Parents may notice a third category of brokenness in a perfectionist child. He or she tends to keep people *away* from them. These children focus on keeping high standards, which they find disappointing in others. They would do whatever they can to be just right in their own eyes without relying on others. He or she prizes a perceived need for self-sufficiency and independence from parents and siblings.

While every child is bent on autonomy, the unhealthy and perfectionist child may simply wish to discard friendships entirely as he or she pursues perfection and the fear of being exposed as imperfect. This child lives in a narrow path of restrictions when it comes to relationships. His or her message is "leave me alone."

On the one hand, the perfectionist child requires less maintenance and is trying to establish excellence in many areas, which often pleases parents. On the other hand, he or she needs to embrace the sorrow that life requires risk and mutually enhancing relationships in God's plan for his or her life's calling to contribute to society.

The perfectionist child must come to terms with grace in order to experience joy in the Holy Spirit. This child may become a decent looking willow, but the flowing streams may not flow into the child if he or she lives out of self-sufficiency. This child must come to own the good news of God's acceptance, even as Christ exposes his or her imperfections, without being afraid of the exposure of guilt and shame. Inviting the perfectionist child into a community of grace and mutual dependency may feel like death for the child, but it is the way of life.

If these three foolish approaches are not addressed with discipline and Gospel wisdom, the parents may be shocked when the compliant child gives into another perceived rescuer, the aggressive child achieves at the expense of a solid relationships with parents and people, and the perfectionist child hardens his or her heart to the Gospel and determines to live a lonely existence independent from Gospel community.

Here is a Gospel prayer parents can have their children memorize based on the doctrine of justification. Pray this: "Father, I am pardoned of all my sins and accepted as righteous in Your sight, but only for the righteousness of Christ imputed to my account and received by faith alone. Amen." Pray that memory will lead to meditation, and meditation to believing prayer and freedom to love well.

So children are asking questions from parents, which must be answered with both tenderness and strength. Children are prone to foolish strategies in their way of relating to parents, which must be disrupted with Gospel wisdom. Often it is the parents, who need the Gospel when it comes to discipline because they may not be aware how discipline is not about the right methods as it is about God's wisdom.

Three Ways Parents Discipline Wrongly

Mere methods of discipline may not address the foolish strategies of children. Children who experience the best of discipline methodology may be shaped to appear behaviorally fine, but may never grow to delight in the Gospel or experience Gospel transformation. Some of the ways children parent wrongly is by angry inflictions of pain such as spankings and beatings, lazy "time outs," and emotional withdrawals.

The problem with angry spankings and beatings is that it does not impart God's wisdom, and only strength is experienced and not tenderness. Since the problem in scripture is a child's folly, inflicting painful consequences merely restrains a child's behavior without Gospel transformation and longer discussions about God, the Gospel, and the way of wisdom. A parent who is slow to anger can use anger in a constructive manner to linger with the disobedient child. Children need God's law, but only to see their need for grace; to behold what Christ did for them in order to supply an endless supply of grace.

"Time out" is a method of discipline where a disobedient child is sent up to his or her room (an isolated place) until the parent lets the child return and continue an activity again. This also is not a recommended method of discipline because it leaves a child isolated with his or her own thoughts. Again, this approach does not impart God's wisdom or offer the Gospel, and may reveal a parent's laziness when it comes to imparting wisdom. Raising children into Gospel maturity requires that they learn about the nature of God's justice, love, and mercy through Jesus Christ.

Hasty spankings done in anger and "time outs" without patient instruction are as unprofitable as emotional withdrawals. When a parent withdraws emotionally from his or her child for misbehavior, the child feels terrible, especially the compliant child. The silent treatment truly inflicts pain, but lacks the much need interpretation about what happened and how people feel.

When a parent withdraws emotionally the aggressive child and the perfectionist child may view their parents' distance as a reason to reinforce their determination to be more independent. A compliant child will experience dread and attempt better behavior without growing in wisdom. After the emotional withdrawal is over suddenly the children realize the parent(s) is okay with them again, but there is no explanation, no reconciliation, nor wisdom given from the parent! These three wrong approaches miss the greatest opportunity for imparting Gospel wisdom into children. What is the purpose of discipline?

Disciplining Children Presents Awesome Opportunities for imparting Wisdom

There is no better time to take your time than when your children disobey. There is no better time to pour wisdom into a child's heart, and to show love, than when we keep our word about the painful consequences in response to misbehavior and rebellious attitudes. Therefore, we must not miss these opportunities by hastily inflicting painful consequences with no loving dialogue, little of patience, and the absence of wise instruction. A parent's strength is discipline is a set up for the parent's tenderness to impart wisdom into a child caught in a moment of folly.

Every child will come to say one thing: "I fail so often." Think about how hard it is to be a child – to know how to understand cultural norms and ethical standards, how to hold a glass of milk without spilling, how to dress and clean up a room, and how to interpret unknown words and strange people. In this developmental process parents must discern between willful rebellion and simple childlike ignorance. It is hard to be a child, and showing grace and kindness always empowers a child. Children want parents to listen, to hear the twofold cry of their hearts.

Children caught in folly are asking the two questions on an ongoing basis; namely, "Do you love me?" and "Can I have my own way?" The latter may or may not be answered in the affirmative, but everyone must learn that our Father God knows what is best for our lives. We must each learn this life lesson. We all must surrender to the will of a parent to say that we do not know what is best for our lives – to learn to trust God when we may not have our own way.

These periodic, unplanned times of discipline are pregnant with opportunity for God to pour out His love, wisdom, and Gospel into our children's lives through parents who are both strong and tender. Here are some practical thoughts to consider.

First, a few household rules like no fits or temper-tantrums and a basic understanding that there can be no privileges without responsibilities are sufficient. Young kids can't handle more than three rules, in my opinion. Besides, once a child exercises self-control in one area, many other responsibilities will be affected.

Second, children will learn that you love them when you keep your word and inflict the sting of painful consequences – whether it is the sting of a small wooden kitchen spoon on the bottom or the removal of a privilege the child longed for. Often your children will see another child in a store throwing a fit, and say: "Daddy, doesn't that kid's parents love their child?" Parents love their children when a few rules are enforced in order to save their child from public embarrassment, and even from dangerous traffic and people. The child will rest secure under you're the parent's care because of the faithful exercise of the parent's word that there will be painful consequences for misbehavior.

Third, the goal is never to simply change behavior. Rather, it is always to pour forth wisdom into your children. These times are the best opportunities to talk about life, love, sin, and redemption. Our best conversations with our children took place in the privacy of my home office. The children shared all kinds of feelings, untrue thoughts that needed to be taken captive, and longings for justice, mercy, and faithfulness.

Justice, mercy, and faithfulness are the only three virtues that Jesus wanted the self-righteous to go and ponder. These three should be the major portion of your conversations when you drive in your car with children, put them to bed, or wake them up in the morning. The main virtues are the plain ones when it comes to the children's conflicts with parents and other siblings. So enforce a few household rules, keep your word about painful consequences, and pour forth wisdom into your children during these times until the most important matters of the law surface; namely, justice, mercy, and faithfulness.

Fourth, parental patience is beautiful. There's no hurry. The patience of a father and a mother, rather than provoking children to anger, will melt their children's hearts. A prompt response to the child's disobedience should be done in slow motion with the single, loving motive of pouring wisdom into the child. Sit down in a private room. Ask questions so that your response is not foolish (Proverbs 18:1,13). It is a perfect moment to slowly dialogue, listen, talk, and instruct.

I miss these times, and delight to watch my five children do this with our grandchildren. Parental patience in one direction towards applying painful consequences and imparting Gospel wisdom to their children is so beautiful, even in the eyes of children. Being slow to anger like God makes your dear children feel secure, knowing that you are just, merciful, and faithful in patiently applying wisdom, love, and protective measures. Parents that rush to inflict impatiently without instruction and a listening ear lose their best opportunities as a parent.

There is no better time for you to take your time than when your children disobey. There is no better time for parents to pour wisdom into a child's heart, and to show love, than when parents keep their word about the painful consequences in response to misbehavior and rebellious attitudes.

Therefore, parents must not miss these opportunities by hastily inflicting painful consequences without loving dialogue, plenty of patience, and wise instruction. What is the weightiest content of wisdom that parents are to impart?

Only Three Weightiest Matters: Justice, Mercy, and Faithfulness

Christian parents are often guilty of raising little, self-righteous Pharisees whom Jesus accused of majoring on the minors. One of the major obstacles for children ending well has been the level of hypocrisy among their peers from Christian families in church and school. "Woe to you, scribes and Pharisees, hypocrites! For you tithe mint and dill and cumin, and have neglected the weightier matters of the law: justice and mercy and faithfulness. These you ought to have done, without neglecting the others" (Matthew 23:23).

If parents require too many rules that major on the minors, then parents will exasperate their children over the least important matters. "Do not exasperate your children" (Ephesians 6:4). We must not provoke our children to anger by an over-demanding approach to parenting. By majoring in the minors we fail to raise our children on "the weightier matters" of the bible; namely, justice, mercy, and faithfulness.

When I was in seminary the Lord convicted me that Karen and I were neglecting the weightier matters on God's heart with our children, and in an ethics class God spoke to me from Jesus' words to the Pharisees. So, I came home and wrote these three words on our front door; "Justice, mercy, and faithfulness." This emphasis on what matters most in a child's behavior became our main emphasis for the years that followed. How do these three weighty virtues relate to discipline?

Justice motivated by Love: Inflicting Painful Consequences and Limits

Parents imitate God when they emphasize justice in their home, especially with their children. God warns us in the bible that there are consequences to our choices. "What you sow you will reap" (Galatians 6:7). God's justice is motivated by love. He is just to forgive us our sins, and loving to discipline His children (1 John 1:9; Hebrews 12:6). Inflicting painful consequences when household rules are not obeyed ought to become a beautiful part of raising children into Gospel maturity. Although painful in the moment, afterwards it yields the peaceful fruit of righteousness (Hebrews 12:11). It requires both strength and tenderness, especially justice and fairness motivated by love.

Taking your time with the child in private to review the transgression and the child's knowledge of what was done can make a big difference, and following through with a painful consequence is a matter of justice. It is often harder on the parents to inflict a painful consequence because of their love for their children, especially when the child is repentant and sorrowful for disobeying. A spank or a grounding teaches children that there are just consequences to their wrong behavior. This is a perfect time to explain the necessity of Christ's death on the cross and how He paid the penalty for our sins, which cannot compare to what our sins truly deserve. Often these conversations become memorable lessons, which lead up to a child's conversion to Christ.

Times of discipline teach justice and fairness. Justice demands that what has been broken or mistreated ought to be restored by the offender. The child's offended sibling or neighbor must experience a restoration and reconciliation process of some sort. Children who grow up where there is an emphasis on justice find security and more peace with parents and siblings than homes where justice is less important, inconsistent, and not motivated by love.

Mercy in Conflicts: Reconciliation with God and Each Other

As children learn of God's justice and learn that there are consequences to their wrong behavior, God's mercy can be taught in wonderful ways. For example, going over the act of disobedience and helping the child to bravely face the painful consequence can be used as a set up for teaching children to love mercy. Some times after our children acknowledged their disobedience and prepared for the consequences of discipline, I would explain that on that one occasion I was going to give them mercy. The surprise look on their faces was a sight for sore eyes. After I explained the Gospel that Jesus took the penalty for our sins, our children would say, "I love mercy!" Often the next time they were disobedient they would ask for mercy, which was offered sparingly.

Mercy involves reconciliation and forgiveness. Children must reconcile with siblings, parents, and those they offended that peace may return to the family. Forgiveness must always be announced by the parents, and requested by the parents when necessary. Offended siblings must offer forgiveness so that the whole family learns to love mercy. Mercy received leads to mercy given, and Jesus often told the Pharisees to go and ponder this: "I delight in mercy not sacrifice" (Matthew 9:13).

Justice and mercy are weighty virtues on Christ's heart for parents to emphasize in the home, and there is one more; faithfulness.

Faithfulness in the Little Things: Routines and Manners

If justice requires courage to act upon consistently in the home and mercy becomes a frequent delight in a family where peace is maintained, then faithfulness is a matter of cultivation a lifestyle of abundant living. Faithfulness is what parents love to see in their children, especially when parents are not around. To hear of how your children were faithful from other parents when you were not present is to realize a major aim in parenting; children who are faithful in the little things. Parents who instruct and train their children to be faithful in little things will prepare their children to succeed in their future callings, and a fitting reward for faithful children is an increase in privileges to be faithful in more. Parents teach faithfulness in little things so that when our children are raised they will be faithful with much. A little thing is a little thing, but faithfulness in a little thing is a big thing. Jesus said:

> One who is faithful in a very little is also faithful in much, and One who is dishonest in a very little thing is also dishonest in much. If then you have not been faithful in the unrighteous wealth, who will entrust to you the true riches? And if you have not been faithful in the use of that which is another's, who will give you that which is your own? (Luke 16:10-12)

This is an excellent passage to meditate upon because Jesus teaches that there are matters more righteous than money, and "riches" to steward worth far more and more true. Cultivating faithfulness in children through the use of money and property, routine chores, good manners, and many other areas of life can become precious lessons about righteousness and true riches.

Justice, mercy, and faithfulness are the weightiest matters of God's Word when it comes to making the most of Gospel discipline, but Gospel discipline's weightiest virtue is love. Parents can both train children to love and practice love for their children in two ways – promoting love of siblings and love of parents when older children do not respond to discipline.

Playing Second Fiddle: the Discipline of Building Others Up

One of the best ways to teach love is to teach it in the context of the home year after year at birthdays and special days like Mother's Day and Father's Day celebrations. One practice in our home was "the discipline of playing second fiddle." W made every birthday celebration an occasion to practice love; "the discipline of playing second fiddle." The celebrated child's siblings helped prepared the meal, set the table, made and gave wrapped presents for their brother or sister, and also spoke a word of appreciation for him or her around the table.

Practicing love by training each child to give preference to one another in honor forces them to give up their foolish strategies. It breaks down walls, pride, and unholy competition. The compliant child must come to the party like the older brother in Jesus' parable (Luke 15) to celebrate the less compliant brother. The aggressive child must learn to honor and love others without competition. The perfectionist child learns the value of community and grace by honoring siblings and coming out of his or her shell.

After the meal and the delicious birthday cake, we went around the table and each of us took turns saying what we appreciate about the celebrated birthday child. This would last a long time. There were, and still are, tears, laughter, and memorable stories. In this way the celebrated child learned to receive love from others and to see how valuable he or she is in the family's larger story. The other children learned to keep the focus off themselves that day by actively serving and speaking edifying words of affirmation to the celebrated sibling or parent. It teaches the discipline of edifying another – "playing second fiddle."

Raising children into Gospel maturity requires parents to remove the folly bound up in their children's hearts through consistent, loving discipline. This chapter shed biblical light on the nature and purpose of discipline by reflecting on the two primary questions children are asking their parents, right and wrong ways to practice discipline, different forms of discipline, the three weightiest matters of discipline, and practical ways love must abound when it comes to discipline. One of the most difficult challenges parents face is the call to love an older child when every effort to discipline doesn't seem to have worked. What does it mean for a parent to love their child well during such a season?

Keeping the Bridge

Sometimes parents find themselves in a difficult season when an older child has not been responding to the Gospel, and in this season the child's folly seems to create a major strain on the relationship with his or her parents. One-way parents can show that they are determined for love to win, for mercy to triumph over judgment, is to "keep the bridge." When parents or friends discover a loved one has trouble embracing their true identity in Christ and are ruled by Satan's lies, it is important to "keep the bridge."

Our tendency is to want to either stand up and fight or hit the road in flight, angry attacks with strong arguments or cutting off the relationship altogether. Parents can use their thirty years of experience at fighting against their child's fifteen years and win absolutely nothing or they can emotionally withdraw in self-protection like a two-year old because they didn't get their way. These strategies function under the illusion of control; that desires have become demands. These ways refuse sorrow, and their anger functions to block the sorrow of unmet longings. Both fight and flight strategies neglect the third way; namely, the way of love. Loving the child requires us to remain in the tension, embrace the sorrow of unmet longings, and seek God's wisdom and salvation in ways that are much more difficult than parents had previously imagined.

Sometimes it is a gender crisis in the child wherein internal confusion makes it difficult for the child to embrace what feels odd and goes against strong urges for same-sex attraction. Maybe the child needs "vitamin M or F" (masculine or feminine involvement and nurturing), but it isn't the end of the story. This does not have to be the last chapter in the parent-child drama because the Gospel offers another chapter in the future and ends in eternity. Fear, regret, children, or anger must not rule parents. Keeping the bridge requires trusting God with desires for the child, hoping in the redemption of all that has gone wrong, and remaining in the tension by being warmly present to love the child well.

Sometimes the loved one embraces a condemning thought; i.e. "I'm a loser or worthless or unlovable." Your Gospel presence and gentle reminders of their justification and adoption in Christ may free them from Satan's lies. When you stay warmly present to them and embrace the sorrow, you will have much more honest and productive conversations that often lead to redemptive results. Soon this dear child may walk over the bridge to solid ground again.

Dr. Dobson then shared about Pete Maravich's testimony, who was a well-known basketball player dying in 1988 at the age of 40 at a basketball court before going to be on Dr. Dobson's radio program, "Focus On The Family" later that day. A year later, Dr. Dobson had a heart attack at the same basketball court.

That is when Dr. Dobson shared a private moment with his son, Ryan and told him that the most important accomplishment in anybody's life is to be in Heaven with the rest of his family. Dr. Dobson said that he would be waiting for his daughter and son. That gave me chills as I listened, as that is my exact thoughts for my own precious family and grandchildren. I will be waiting for them in Heaven.

There is nothing that money can buy or that my children, their spouses or grandchildren could accomplish in their lifetime than to finish their life walking close to their Lord and Savior Jesus Christ, being Heaven bound and to finish

the race marked out for each one of them. Dr. Dobson
said to his son, "Ryan, Be There!"

Dr. Dobson suffered a heart attack and was in the hospital
for almost two weeks. This gave him a long time to reflect
on the things in life that were important to him. Not long
after he was released from the hospital, he sat down and
had a talk with his college-aged son Ryan. His words
went something
like this:

> Ryan. I had a heart attack. I didn't die, but I sure
> could have. You didn't have to bury me this time.
> But, unless the Lord returns soon or you suffer an
> untimely death, there will come a day when you
> will have to bury me. Chances are you will see me
> die. But this I know. When I die, I will be called
> up to be with my Lord on the other side. And
> Ryan, I will be waiting for you. I will be looking
> for you. Ryan, BE THERE!!! Nothing else
> matters. I hope you live a life of fulfillment as I
> have. I hope you find a wonderful wife and have
> beautiful children. I hope your life is filled with
> many blessings as mine has been. But all of this
> doesn't matter in comparison to being there on the
> other side. Whatever it takes, whatever happens,
> BE THERE! Ryan, that's all that really matters.
> Please, BE THERE!!![xxii]

Well, this father delivered the mail, and his son received
it one subsequent day after. When a child goes astray,
remember to be slow to anger and patient in your

desperation. There is always hope that the child will "be there."

Children require discipline because of the necessity to remove folly bound up in their heart. Parents communicate both strength and tenderness in answering the two fundamental questions their children are asking: "Am I loved?" and "Can I have my own way?" This chapter shed biblical light on the nature and purpose of discipline, presented some right and wrong ways to practice disciplining children, exposed some foolish strategies of children, emphasized the weightiest matters of discipline, and gave practical wisdom to train and practice loving well in the good times and the most difficult ones.

Christian parenting is a privileged calling that begins with vision and requires a warm presence to establish children's identity, a sure promise to trust God for, a surprising posture to live before God, and a solid commitment to practice loving and consistent discipline in imparting wisdom. Christian parenting is also a matter of fulfilling the Great Commission; namely, making disciples. The next chapter shows how Christian parenting is life on life, missional discipleship.

Discussion Questions

1. What are the two basic questions children ask? How are you, in general, answering them?

2. Of the three wrong ways children approach parents, which one describes your child?

3. What is the purpose of discipline? What improvements do you need to make in discipline times with your child?

4. What are the three primary virtues that Jesus gave the most weight to with regard to discipleship (parenting), and which of the three – love, mercy, and faithfulness – stood out to you as the one you want to emphasize more in discipline times?

5. How have you helped your child learn "to play second fiddle" before other children?

6. What does it mean to "keep the bridge" with your children? Why is this so important, and yet so difficult for a parent?

Chapter Five: Life on Life Missional Discipleship

Hear, O Israel: The LORD our God, the LORD is one.
You shall love the LORD your God with all your heart and
with all your soul and with all your might. And these
words that I command you today shall be on your
heart. You shall teach them diligently to your
children, and shall talk of them when you sit in
your house, and when you walk by the way, and
when you lie down, and when you rise. You shall
bind them as a sign on your hand, and they shall
be as frontlets between your eyes. You shall write
them on the doorposts of your house and on your
gates (Deuteronomy 6:4-9).

Whereas the previous chapter was about the subject of
discipline, this chapter is similar because the word
discipline is like the word *discipleship*. Followers of
Christ in the New Testament were known as disciples of
Christ, and were first called *Christians* in Antioch (Acts
11:25). When we taught our children beginning Latin they
learned the word *disciplulas*, which means student or
disciple. Children of believers are disciples called to come
to Christ for rest and take up their cross and follow Christ
with their parents. Christ offers both rest and a costly life.

This chapter describes parenting in the context of
discipleship – a life on life way of parental instruction
with an aim motivated by mission. It includes the matter
of Christian education, which covers all of life, even such
subjects as reading, imagination, creation, sports, arts,
language, scripture, catechism, theology, sanctification,
sexuality, and maturity so that children may grow into

Gospel maturity and become like *willows by flowing streams.*[xxiii]

Parenting is Life on Life Missional Discipleship

When Jesus called His first disciples, as He calls us today, He spoke the simple words, "Follow Me" (Mark 1:17; 2:14; John 1:43). Parents are instruments of Christ to speak His voice and call to discipleship, calling their children into an intimate, instructive, and imitative relationship with our master teacher; namely, Jesus Christ.

Disciples of Christ, parents, are under a mandate to make disciples and disciple-makers because He commands His disciples to "Go into all the world and make disciples" (Matthew 28:18-20). This is called the "Great Commission," and it begins in the home with Christian parents and their children.

In the establishment of God's redeemed people, redeemed out of slavery to the Egyptians by the blood of the lamb, God put the burden of discipleship on the parents involved in the believing community. Parenting is life on life discipleship lived out in the context of the local church today. Notice the words commanded to the parents in Deuteronomy imply a life on life enterprise, not an ancient Greek or American classroom pedagogy or method of education. "You shall teach them diligently to your children, and shall talk of them when you sit in your house, and when you walk by the way, and when you lie down, and when you rise." Life on life is more than words spoken from parents to children, for we often agree at some level that more is caught than taught. It involves a constant, living conversation about how to apply God's Word in all of life – when you sit in your house, and when you walk or drive on the way, and when you lie down, and when you rise.

Sitting in Your Home

Sitting at home, parents are engaged in discipleship with their children. The bible is opened and taught to give an understanding of the various genres of scripture, from narratives of Genesis in the lives of the patriarchs and Joseph to the comedy romance narrative of Ruth. The Proverbs, the Psalms, Job, and Ecclesiastes offer God's wisdom about the way things are in God's created and fallen world. The prophets teach the way of catching the hard heart in sin, and the priestly ways of inviting those caught in sin can come into God's presence for acceptance and grace. The kings teach us how to, and how not to, lead, defend, and prosper in order to bring peace and justice. All three Old Testament offices of prophet, priest, and king are fulfilled in Christ, who is the Prophet, Great High Priest, and King of kings.

Sitting in your home, children are invited into discipleship as they read the four gospels, which goes out of its' way to show that all disciples fail to follow perfectly and are in need of the Gospel of grace. Matthew is the "sinner" and tax thief, who Jesus came to seek when he was unrighteous (Matthew 9:9-13). Peter makes sure that John tells of his unfaithful and threefold denial of Jesus so that disciples discover Christ's grace of restoring a disciple into leadership after a fall (John 21).

Paul, the enemy of Christ and the disciples, is converted and becomes a display of how the worst of sinners is shown God's mercy in Jesus Christ (Acts 9; 1 Timothy 1:15). Paul and Timothy's mother and grandmother make Timothy a disciple of Christ through sitting in his home and Paul's. Sitting in your home is the place of discipleship where children hear the invitation of Christ, "Come to Me for rest, and follow Me."

Walking by the Way

Life on life discipleship takes place "when you walk by the way." We don't walk much in our culture, but a walk in a park or a drive in the car or van is implied today. When our children were young, I took the three older children on my four-mile runs. They rode on their bikes. Emily had the largest bike, Nate rode a smaller one, and Jonathan rode a little one with training wheels. I would catechize them, listen to their hearts and stories, and we had a great time together. They enjoyed getting outside and being with me, but I made running by the way a matter of discipleship. I wanted to redeem the time by investing in their lives.

One day on a ride it became evident that there was sibling rivalry, comparisons and competition among the three children. When we came home from "walking by the way," we "sat in our home." As we sat around the kitchen table, I lead them in a discussion aimed at recognizing that they each had tremendous gifts. They were able to see how differently they were gifted, and how God had arranged their order of age and put them together as a family. The family, I explained, was the place of discipleship to prepare them for when they were on their own as adults. As they learned the principles of loving well and appreciating each other in love, they would be prepared to do the same in their future places of home and calling. There were a lot of tears as we embraced the sorrow of each one's limitations and longings, and there was laughter as we embraced our weaknesses too. It was a kairotic[xxiv] moment that shaped their lives, and mine, for years to come. In this sense it was missional. If I had not taught them "by the way," I would not have had the life-changing moment with them in "sitting in the home."

When you Lie Down

Discipleship takes place also "when you lie down." Bedtime, in my opinion, is one of the best places to invest in life on life discipleship. We would lie down alongside each child's bed and soon their questions would arise out of their hearts. Sometimes I did not have perfect answers to questions like, "How can God always be?" It is hard to grasp God is eternal. The children would dream about what they wanted to be when they grew up, or they often shared how others hurt their feelings that day. All manner of subjects were discussed, and in the end I would place my hand on their heads and bless them in God's Name for a bright future.

When you Rise

Christian parenting is life on life discipleship "when you sit in your home, or walk by the way, and when you lie down, and when you rise." In the morning when we rose from sleep, and a new day meant starting all over again.

How do you teach your children "when you rise?" Isn't it freeing to create your own schedule for discipleship? There is no one method, but we are free to use creativity to make the most of each morning. We taught them when they arose in a variety of ways over the years. When they were young we sang a hymn of praise and simply enjoyed each other's company. For one season we home-schooled, and at other chapters of life the children went to private and public schools. In the private Christian schools they went to chapel services, and when we educated them at home they joined in a devotional. Karen got ready for the day during the home-school years, and I would lead them in love, Latin, and logic. Love was theology and bible, and the other subjects are self-explanatory. When parents rise in the morning we have a responsibility to make the most of this time to disciple children.

We loved our time on "love." Teaching them to love God and shaping their character to love others well was mixed with fun. If they answered a catechism question correctly, they each could perform a feat like a summersault or a leap on the couch, and it ended with a piece of candy as a reward. They were instructed in theology, bible, and the *Children's Catechism of the Westminster Confession of Faith*. I also taught them from *The Dictionary of Cultural Literacy* on idioms to make the logic portion more interesting. When I was through with "love," Latin, and logic, Karen would be ready to teach all the other important subjects.

Discipleship, according to Deuteronomy 6, takes place sitting in the home, walking by the way, lying down at night, and rising in the morning. Discipleship is a matter of educating children to become followers of Christ.

Christian Education

Parents educate and disciple children in reading, imagination, creation, science, math, grammar, history, sports, arts, language, scripture, economics, sexuality, and theology. Financial stewardship, for example, begins in the home. Parents, who budget, tend to train their children to do the same, especially in teen years. Evidently, many parents are not preparing their children to spend and save money responsibly. For example, 35% of the Ameriprise study parents said their kids had not mastered even the *basics* of financial responsibility. Their kids were also polled, and 56% of them said their parents had never talked about budgeting or saving. Just 11% of surveyed adult children said they had been advised to "expect the unexpected."[xxv] We also taught on sexuality one on one in privacy.

Sex education, to take another example, is best taught by parents. As chapter one explained, children should be taught the glory and ruin of being male or female. This will lead to answering the question: what does a redeemed man and woman look like? Sex education is so important, and there are Christian resources for parents on this subject fashioned according to the child's age level.[xxvi] I was the parent who usually taught this subject to each child one on one, life on life. Although it is kind of awkward for both the child and the parent, it is vital that children receive God's interpretation and perspective on sexuality from their parents before our contemporary culture through friends and social media offer another perspective. After this, and along the way towards Gospel maturity, it is helpful for parents to teach the children to discern the various ways our culture and other cultures interpret and place values on sexuality.

In this life on life process of discipleship parents are aiming for Gospel maturity in their children so that they become like *willows by flowing streams*. Parents with such a vision have an aim to life on life discipleship, a missional nature to this process. Children are like arrows in the quiver of a parent (Psalm 127). A parent must not become "a helicopter parent," whose message is: "You can't live without me!" This message translated actually means: "I can't live without you." Dependent parenting leads to enmeshment with the child, but life on life discipleship pulls back the bow with aim and tension to shoot our children towards a target for the glory of God.

I recently read about "Mrs. Fidget" in C.S. Lewis' book *The Four Loves*. This fictitious woman's death changed her frowning husband to a man who could laugh again, her son from "an embittered, peevish little creature" to become quite human, her daughter from a delicate girl to one who "dances all night" and plays tennis, and her dog too. "Even the dog who was never allowed out except on a lead," Lewis wrote, "is now a well-known member of the Lamp-post Club in their road."

Mrs. Fidget "lived for her family" – washing, cleaning, cooking, and staying up late to greet her children with a silent accusation. She made things the family did not want to wear, and cooked meals they soon despised. Why? She needed to be needed to feel her worth, but "then a love like Mrs. Fidget's contains a good deal of hatred."

If you are a "Mrs. Fidget," who needs to be needed for a sense of worth, you are using your children for your self-worth and theirs as you "work your fingers to the bone." What would it mean for you as a parent to rest secure in your worth so that your motives for serving your children are more purely out of love for them? Lewis concludes:

> The Vicar says Mrs. Fidget is now at rest. Let us hope she is. What's quite certain is that her family are . . . We feed children in order that they may soon be able to feed themselves; we teach them in order that they may soon not need our teaching . . . The hour when we can say "They need me no longer" should be our reward.[xxvii]

What's your aim? Is it to send your children out able to live independently from you? In general, parents are training children in the way they each should go so that when they are old they will not depart from it. We are aiming, on the whole, towards Gospel maturity, and one of the best ways to invest in our children in life on life discipleship is through taking each one on an occasional "date."

Taking Your Child on a Date

A date is not romantic like a husband taking his wife on a date, as you already know. Rather, it is about love between a parent and a child or a grandchild. Taking a daughter or a son on a date involves spending one-on-one-time with each child. This practice over the years has proven to be one of the most fruitful means of discipleship for parents to make a permanent mark on their lives for Christ.

An ambassador for Great Britain, Mr. Adams, was so busy trying to be important in his work that he did not consider a date with his son a good investment of his time. One day he took his son fishing. His son, Brooks Adams, wrote in his journal, "I went fishing with my Dad. It was the most glorious day of my life." His father wrote in his own journal, "'Went fishing with my son – a day wasted." Little did he realize that his son would speak of that day for the next forty years as the most significant day of his childhood. C. S. Lewis wrote, "Fatherhood must be the core of the universe."[xxviii]

I would often have one major concern for the child on a date, but I learned to wait and just listen to the child for the beginning time and quite a ways through our time together. We might listen to their favorite music on the way for an ice cream or to camp out, but sooner or later each child would share with some tears or laughter what was happening in their life. Issues, which a parent would never have known without taking them out on dates, will come to the surface. Dates offer golden opportunities to offer sympathetic love and the truths of the Gospel. These times become the occasion to put forth a challenge to further surrender the children's lives to Christ and follow Christ more fully.

Discipleship is a process of becoming more committed to Christ and to surrender our wills to His plan for our lives. As C. S. Lewis put it,

> The terrible thing, the almost impossible thing, is to hand over your whole self – all your wishes and precautions – to Christ. But it is far easier than what we are all trying to do instead . . . to remain what we call 'ourselves.'[xxix]

Discipleship is a matter of losing yourself for Jesus' sake in order to find a new self and identity in Him, and taking your child on a date has a purposeful nature to it because parenting is life on life missional discipleship.

Helping Children Count the Cost of Discipleship

Parenting children towards Christ is a matter of going against our child's natural bent. It requires a parent to lose their children for Jesus' sake in order to keep them. It requires a parent to find their identity in Christ rather than finding their identity in their children. It is parenting on mission for the sake of Christ's mission to change the world as we know it. Therefore, parents are leading their children where they do not want to go – to the nursery, to school, and to lay down their lives for Christ. Jesus said to Peter: "Truly, truly, I say to you, when you were young, you used to dress yourself and walk wherever you wanted, but when you are old, you will stretch out your hands, and another will dress you and carry you where you do not want to go" (John 21:18).

Parents are often called to lead children where they do not want to go. For example, Corrie Ten Boom explains how this happened with her Christian father. After the older children ran off for school from the breakfast table where Corrie Ten Boom's father had finished the morning devotional, the five remaining adults realized Corrie was the only child still seated at the table. She did not want to go to school. Corrie records her memory in *The Hiding Place* of what happened next:

> "Corrie!" cried Mama. "Have you forgotten you're a big girl now? Today you go to school too! Hurry, or you must cross the street alone!" Corrie replied: "I'm not going." Corrie explained, "There was a short, startled silence, broken by everybody at once, but Father's deep voice drowned them out." Her father said: "Of course she's not going alone! Nollie was excited today and forgot to wait, that's all. Corrie is going with me."

Corrie recalled being lead where she did not want to go by her father:

> "And with that he took my hat from its peg, wrapped my hand in his, and led me from the room. My hand in Father's! That meant the windmill on the Spaarne River, or swans on the canal. But this time he was taking me where I didn't want to go!

There was a railing along the bottom five steps: I grabbed it with my free hand and held on. Skilled watchmaker's fingers closed over mine and gently unwound them.

Howling and struggling, I was led away from the world I knew into a bigger, stranger, harder one."...[xxx]

Sometimes our loving Father takes us by the hand to places in life we do not want to go. Sometimes they are bigger, sometimes smaller, often stranger, and often bigger. We may cling to old places and seasons of security with white knuckles, but God is stronger and able to separate our grip and take us where we should go next. We may find ourselves howling and struggling, but with determined love our Father takes us to places we do not want to go.

I did not want to go to the place God called me to pastor, at least not for long. For the next twenty years He would gently unwind my finger off my grip upon other places. After twenty-five years of serving here, I am grateful that He took me by the hand to a place I did not want to go. We did not want to face the deaths of both our parents and our granddaughter, but He took us by the hand to places of mourning on many occasions. Now, we are glad He did, for they are better for healing and wisdom's sake than houses of laughter.

Sometimes our Father takes us by the hand to places we do not want to go because He is authoring a better Gospel story than we can write about redeeming our tragedies. God calls parents, like Corrie's father, to a life on life missional discipleship relationship in order that they would lead their children into a fallen world to suffer for the sake of Christ's mission and others' welfare. This is the way to joy and fulfillment, surprisingly this is what we shall discover in the end.

This chapter described discipleship in the context of parenting – a life on life way of discipleship with an aim motivated by mission. It included the matter of Christian education, which covers all of life, even such subjects as reading, imagination, creation, sports, arts, language, scripture, catechism, theology, sanctification, sexuality, and maturity so that children may *grow into Gospel maturity* and become like *willows by flowing streams*. The next chapter, like this chapter, involves all of life. It is a call for parents to ascribe worth to God in that context of home, callings, and church; namely, teaching children to worship God.

Discussion Questions

1. How is parenting a matter of life on life, missional discipleship? When does discipleship begin and end in our day-to-day experience? In what ways could you be more intentional to disciple your children during the ordinary events of a day?

2. What aspects of education would you like to become more involved in with your child's education? Have you taught your child on gender and sex education?

3. What do think about taking your child out on a one on one date together? How might this be helpful for each parent?

4. What occasions do you recall when you had to lead your child where she or he did not want to go? How will this benefit the child in the future?

Chapter Six: Worship

The ESV bible heading, "Rules for Christian Households," begins:

> Wives, submit to your husbands, as is fitting in the Lord. Husbands, love your wives, and do not be harsh with them. Children, obey your parents in everything, for this pleases the Lord. Fathers, do not provoke your children, lest they become discouraged. Bondservants, obey in everything those who are your earthly masters, not by way of eye-service, as people-pleasers, but with sincerity of heart, fearing the Lord. Whatever you do, work heartily, as for the Lord and not for men, knowing that from the Lord you will receive the inheritance as your reward. You are serving the Lord Christ (Colossians 3:18-24).

In chapter six, like the previous chapter, both discipleship and worship involve all of life. This chapter explains how parents mark their children's view and love of God, and therefore how they express their affections for God in song, prayer, education, and work in the home, church, and culture with their possessions and global concern that all the peoples of the earth give God glory.

Parents Mark Children's View of God

Parenting a child is to parent a worshiper. Therefore, we must always diagnose what is ruling our child's heart and affections. Whether in our homes or in our daily living in our communities, the Christian sees everything they do as an act of worship to Christ. Paul wrote to the Corinthians, "Whether you eat or drink, or whatever you do, do all to glorify God" (1 Corinthians 10:31). Interestingly, he wrote to the Colossians about worship and service to Christ in the context of family – marriage, parenting, and work.

Everything we do as a family reflects our worship of God, whether we are merely attempting to please people as a functional god or serve people to please Christ above. In all of life parents are teaching by word and deed to ascribe worship to God. This includes both our relationships as married couples and as parents with the responsibilities of chores in the home. Worshipping Christ frees us to serve others with meaningful intentions because we are aiming to please God in the ordinary.[xxxi]

Parents teach worship when they consider how to instruct children to steward their possessions and money so that they are not possessed by, but possess them by teaching generosity towards the church, ministries of mercy, and missions. Sharing toys and giving away clothes are simple ways to sense that things we own are not ours, but the Lord's to steward and offer to others in His Name. This keeps a child's heart from idolatry and attachment to things.

Teenagers and their Appearance

Every teen comes to realize that their appearance in our culture matters, especially to other teens. This, too, is can be a way that parents mark children's view of God, and

why looks can either draw people to themselves or the
Lord.

A story is told of a teen with an obvious birthmark
covering his face. It did not bother him the way we might
expect. The boy had a secure sense of his identity in
Christ, had a higher EQ level, and focused on the Lord
and others. When asked by another teen, "Are you aware
there's a large birth defect on your face?," he responded,
"Of course, I am." This question was followed by, "Why
doesn't it bother you in the slightest?" He answered with
a smile, "When I was young my Dad told me it was there
for two reasons. One, because God kissed me there.
Secondly, because Dad could always see me in a crowd."
Then, he continued, "My Dad told me this with so much
love that as I grew up I actually began to feel sorry for the
other kids who weren't kissed like I was." Proverbs says
that the tongue has the power of life and death. This
father's words had the power of life, and used a defect as
a call for worship.

One sign that worship of God is obstructed is when our
child has an inordinate attachment to something or
someone else. It could be a game or a toy, and the
question parents must ask is whether or not their children
can live without them. What or who are they truly living
for? Many times we had to challenge our children's idols.
We did this in a way to put that toy or person in its' place
where it belongs. Children do what they do because of
what they worship. Because of this, Gospel
transformation is not so much about behavior
management, but about Christ being the object of their
worship. Being an instrument of Gospel transformation

means getting at worship issues within your child's motivations.

When we were in seminary my wife Karen put "bunny" – a blanket with a bunny's head on it – into the washing machine. Our son fell prostrate because he could not live without bunny for a few hours. Although this seems like a minor issue, we did not give into our child. Bunny needed to be washed, and no overt act of devotion to bunny was going to rule our lives.

Raising children into Gospel maturity begins even when they are little, but it may be more obvious when they are teens. Paul David Tripp gives a hypothetical illustration of this when he writes:

> Your sixteen-year-old daughter spends what you think is a ridiculous amount of time in the bathroom every morning. She never seems to have enough clothes. She devours fashion magazines and websites. You have begun to think that she must be the selfie queen of her generation. She not only constantly takes selfies, but she also takes selfies in the mirror, so she has selfies of her taking selfies! You are concerned that she puts on too much makeup and wants to dress too provocatively. You are saddened that what she looks like on the outside gets way more attention and concern than what is happening on the inside. As you listen to her talk, you are concerned with how important the reactions of friends (particularly boys) are to her and her appearance. She's constantly telling you that she thinks she's

ugly or fat. She tells you she hates her nose, thinks her calves are too big, and wishes she wasn't so flat-chested. With all her attention on her appearance, she frets every time she goes out and seldom seems happy for very long.[xxxii]

What is going on in this teenage girl's life has to do with worship. Who has she given the authority to tell her who she is? Apparently, she is not receiving the Gospel of acceptance, righteousness, and love from the Lord, which she ought to receive on the front end of every day. She shifted her heart to find acceptance and love in a lesser god, and she performs for her functional god, whether she is a Christian or not. What is motivating her to get up and help her face and well-being each day?

Helping her embrace the sorrow of unmet longings for acceptance from others will enable her to see who she has attached her identity and the security to that cannot, and will not, deliver her. In her lack of heart's rest in her identity in Christ, she became all the more addicted and obsessed. She feels she must concentrate more on, and work harder at, becoming beautiful and attractive to others. Perhaps that will allure the boys to her. She desperately needs life on life discipleship from her parents, who will do more than try to control her outward behavior. She needs parents who understand her at her heart level to see how her performance functions to get what she already has in the Gospel.

This is a matter of worship, not makeup. It is about rest and identity, not whether or not she dresses pretty. She was built for God, and her heart will be restless until she finds her security in Christ each day.

We can live without the many possessions we have, and there is nothing better than taking children on a mission trip to be exposed to poverty. One of our goals was to make sure that we took each child on a mission trip by the time they each reached eighteen years old. We went to nations where the children came face to face with poverty. They experienced serving the poor by building schools and teaching the bible in other cultures within the United States and beyond.

I'll never forget how our youngest daughter longed to be a missionary and marry a "Jim Elliot." When she was in high school she went on a missions trip to South Africa and Zimbabwe. When Lizzy was gone for two weeks in the midst of poverty and the challenges of a new culture to share the Gospel, we were cleaning up her room and picked up Elisabeth Elliot's book on Amy Charmichael entitles *A Chance to Die*. What this discovery of a book exposed was our idolatry of our daughter, Lizzy. Could we live without her if she either moved on the mission field or died when away from her parents?

Worship is an act that takes place in times of suffering. Job said in the midst of suffering, "Though He slay me, yet will I worship Him" (Job 13:15). Worship is best when we are faced with the fact that to die is gain. I'll never forget the phone call Lizzy made to me from Zimbabwe telling me, "Dad, today I saw poverty face to face." We both cried over the phone and, in a sense,

worshipped God in prayer. How do children learn to pray
and worship?

Teaching Your Children to Pray Together

A simple way to practice worship is through song and
prayer where a family gathers in a living room one night a
week or more for worship. We lit a candle, put on our
pajamas, and sat around the beautiful candle. We used the
ACTS acronym to guide us through adoration, confession
(forgiveness), thanksgiving, and supplication. Karen or I
would ask one of the children to begin with: "God You
are (an attribute of God)." One child might begin with a
prayer of adoration, "God You are holy," and then we
each went one at a time in any order for a while adoring
God by various attributes. Then I would ask another child
to begin the next section with "God, forgive me for
(confession of a sin)." Each of us would ask God for
various sins and bad attitudes for a while. Then I asked
another child to pray, "God, I forgive (name of a
person)." Each of us would forgive people we felt
offended us recently, and the people were often simply
someone in our own family. Then, I would ask a child,
because each child loved to begin each new section of
prayer, "God, we thank You for ____." Thanksgiving
would last for a bit before our last section; namely, "God,
I ask for ____."

Before we knew it we had prayed a good, long while. The
peace of God and His presence was enjoyed in a beautiful
way. We would close with a song of worship or two, and
then head up to our beds. Karen and I were usually
amazed at all that came out of our children's hearts that

we simply were unaware of, or surprised by, their love for God.

Worship Times with Older Children

One of the easiest ways we found to continue to worship as a family was when they learned to play guitar. Some evenings after dinner, some games, and laughter, we would gather in the living room and sing praise songs to God together. Then, we would simply take time to pray together. These times are spontaneous and enjoyable because the children were older and did not need much of our input, only our presence and leadership.

Worship involves all of life, but may be particularized in a time of family worship. This chapter explained how parents mark their children's view and love of God, and therefore, how they express their affections for God in song, prayer, generosity, education, and work in the home, church, and global concern that all the peoples of the earth give God glory. The next chapter will emphasize how parents call each child to express their worship in their individual callings and prepare their child to leave home in order to fulfill God's purposes for their lives.

Discussion Questions

1. How does your influence mark your child's view of God? In what ways are you ascribing praise to God with your children?

2. Are you willing to discuss how the Gospel is influencing your child's motivation for dress and performance in sports and music? What is the danger of mere behavioral management?

3. Have you considered going on a mission trip together with your children?

4. What do think about the suggested way of teaching your children to pray together? Have you, or can you envision, singing praise together with your older children?

Chapter Seven: Releasing Arrows by Discerning and Affirming Callings

This is one of my favorite chapters, which is about children learning how to discerning and fulfilling their callings from God, and how parents may help children to discern and affirm their children's callings. It shows the importance of seeing every calling as sacred, not just full-time vocational service as pastors or missionaries. It answers and puts forth a vision for the good life, which is an ordinary and weighty one lived under God's smile. The subjects related to this will include the power of differentiated gender, pronouncing blessings over our children's heads, parenting like God as an eagle parent with eaglets, envisioning an ordinary life as greatness, cultivating a sense of calling through social justice, compassionate service, and humility, the significance of prevocational jobs, embracing longings, and finding their place in our Father's world as disciples engaged in selfless mission for Christ.

The Power of Gender Differentiation

When children reach teenage years they are in need of affirmation and separation, affirmation that God loves them and has a particular call on their lives and separation from their mothers and the milieu of home. Children are in need of a message like, "You are a woman like your mom, but you are not your mom," or "You are a man like your father, but you are not your dad." They would love to hear, "God has a call on your life, and you will be given strength in weakness to fulfill God's purposes for your life."

Mother's give well-being to a child, which helps them rest and know all is secure. Father's give a sense of significance, that the child's life and calling matters for eternity. In teen years, however, tension will begin to exist between children and mom. Parents may notice increased tension and conflict. This is because God has ordained that there must begin a process of separation and differentiation. The father's voice will be important in separating a child from the mother, and calling the child out of the home and into the world for meaningful service. A father's delight in who a child is, and what he or she will become, is essential as the child enters into the calling God has for the child's life outside the home. A mother's voice says, "Come back home and be well," but a father's voice says, "Go out there and go for it because, by God's grace, you can." This is the healthy and necessary process of separation and differentiation.

Blessings for a Bright Future

Karen and I were invited over to have dinner with a large Christian family. The six children behaved well, and the food was delicious. After dinner at a long table, we sat in the living room until the children went to bed. We observed two things that night. First, that the children knew their father would take care of any injustice with loving discipline and wisdom. Second, that the children all wanted a blessing spoken by their father over them.

At one point after dinner in the living room, one of the toddler boys came waddling in with a milk bottle in one hand and a wooden spoon in the other. He wanted his father to spank his brother, but his father informed him that he would take care of the apparent injustice another way. When it was time for bed, the children came in one by one they came to hug and kiss their parents good night, but they also each bowed their heads for their father to place his hand over them an pronounce a benediction or a blessing. It was remarkable. We had never witnessed such a simple and profound parental practice, namely pronouncing benedictions or blessings over one's children each night.

When we drove home that night, Karen and I discussed again how we longed to have large family. I said to Karen, "I can't wait to rest my hand on the heads of each of our children to bless them before bed." It was a practice that I kept until our five children were all married. Now it is their practice too, and we can participate with our children to bless our grandchildren from time to time.

From youth to adulthood parents may bless their children in faith for a meaningful calling and future. This helps the child discover their sense of calling and know that the parent is for their best under God's favor. In other words, a benediction is an effective means of communicating "good things" from God, who is the source of all true blessings, through human instruments God put in authority over others to bless. A benediction is God's blessing conferred on a person or group by God's designated agent. It is only God who effectively blesses; all human blessing is, therefore, intercession with God for His blessing. We speak over another with eyes open, trusting God to fulfill, while God freely bestows His goodness in time.

Although associated with ending a corporate worship setting with a final good word, benedictions are not limited to these times. The word benediction derives from two Latin words that mean, "to speak well of," and people in every culture and generation look earnestly and intently for a final word of divine kindness from God through His ordained agents of blessings; namely, parents and grandparents.

Parents and grandparents have the esteemed privilege from God to bless their children and grandchildren, and often they may not see the effect of their endeavors for many years. Therefore, benedictions are given by faith in hope. They bless the next generation because they are blessed, and they have peace and comfort in speaking well of their children under God's favor. Their blessings may have great results, and often this is the case after they are gone out of the world, as you may imagine. Their children's children unto a thousand generations shall discover on the last day that benedictions mattered.

Write out benedictions to speak to your loved ones with faith, hope, and love. Use biblical language and metaphors. Here is a great resource and some examples from my Old Testament professor at Covenant Theological Seminary, Dr. Robert Vasholz. Vasholz occasionally combines scripture with hymns. Of the many Vasholz provides in his book Benedictions, I have selected eleven.

And now may the God who sought you when a stranger; wandering from the fold of God; Who interposed His precious blood to rescue you from danger. Give you voice to praise Him, for to sing His praises is good, pleasant and becoming all your days.

May you be lost in wonder, love, and praise, so that through every period of your life His goodness you pursue, Until our Lord comes again. Now may the God Who tends and spares us and well knows our feeble frame; Our Father who gently bears us and rescues us from our foes, Establish you like Mt. Zion, which cannot be moved but abides forever.

And now, press on to maturity, With the confidence that what e're God ordains is right, And though dark the road, He holds you that you shall not fall.

To you whose life is hid with Christ on High, Whoever lives and pleas for you; May He keep you from stumbling, And make you to stand in the presence of His glory, Blameless and with great joy.

Now may the God Who tends and spares us and well knows our feeble frame; Our Father who gently bears us and rescues us from our foes, Establish you like Mt. Zion, which cannot be moved but abides forever.

And now, press on to maturity, With the confidence that whate're God ordains is right, And though dark the road, He holds you that you shall not fall.

To you whose life is hid with Christ on High, Whoever lives and pleas for you; May He keep you from stumbling, And make you to stand in the presence of His glory, Blameless and with great joy.

And now to God's elect, Whom He has upheld since they were conceived, Carried since they were born, Hear His good promise; "I am He; I will sustain you, I will carry you, I will rescue even to your old age."

And now may He grace you with his presence, So that the weak might say, "I am strong," And the poor say, "I am rich," And the feeble say, "I am upheld."

May the feeblest among you be like David, May the God who gives encouragement and endurance, Give you the Spirit of unity as you follow Christ, So that with one heart and one mouth we may together, Glorify the God and Father of our Lord Jesus Christ.

From the God Most High, Whose ways are mercy and truth, Who leads you to His heavenly throne. May He preserve your life according to His promise; Keep you from all harm, And watch over

> your life. So that with one heart and one mouth
> we may together, Glorify the God and Father
> of our Lord Jesus Christ.[xxxiii]

Imagine how your loved ones shall feel receiving such good words from you in your last season of spiritual formation when you leave your Gospel legacy. There is no weightier or greater person to speak well of a child than a parent, grandparent, elder, or pastor. We live in a fallen world where curses may easily be spoken from day to day. Curses are the opposite of benedictions and have dreadful effects at times.

Our benedictions can also be prayed to God on behalf of others. Often before I fall asleep, I will renounce any evil curses spoken over any of the heads in our family. I then plead the blood of Christ would cover us. Finally, I pray down every spiritual blessing that is ours in Christ Jesus through the Holy Spirit. What's your message going to be in the last years of your life? Please consider the use of benedictions in leaving a legacy from Christ, which is your life's message.

Parenting takes a long-term view because parenting is a process, and not a one-time event. Your children may recall these years later, like the famous missionary John Paton.

A Father's Last Benediction

John Paton was a missionary to the New Hebrides, today called Vanuatu, in the South Seas. Paton remembers his father's last word, which was backed up by a life's message. Paton remembered with fresh tears on his cheeks how his "dear father" walked with him the first six miles of the way on their parting journey. His father's advice mixed with tears and Christian discussion were still fresh on his heart as if it were but one day before. Paton recalled how his father's lips kept moving in silent prayers for him and how tears welled up in his eyes when their eyes met and talking seemed to be in vain.

When they halted on reaching the final point of departure, he grasped his son's hand firmly for a minute in silence and then solemnly and affectionately said, "God bless you, my son! Your father's God prosper you and keep you from all evil!" Unable to say more, his father's lips kept moving in silent prayer; in tears they embraced, and then they parted ways. Paton wrote, I ran off as fast as I could, and, when about to turn a corner in the road where he would lose sight of me, I looked back and saw him still standing with head uncovered where I had left him. Waving my hat in adieu, I was round the corner and out of sight in an instant. But my heart was too full and sore to carry me further, so I darted into the side of the road and wept for a time. Then, rising up cautiously, I climbed the dyke to see if he yet stood where I had left him, and just at that moment I caught a glimpse of him climbing the dyke and looking out for me! He did not see me, and after he had gazed eagerly in my direction for a while, he got down, turned his face towards home, and began to return— his head still uncovered, and his heart, I felt sure, still rising in prayers for me. I watched

through blinding tears, till his form faded from my
gaze; and then, hastening on my way, vowed
deeply and oft, by the help of God, to live and act
so as never to grieve or dishonor such a father and
mother as He had given me.[xxxiv]

God is like a Parent Eagle

Like an eagle that stirs up its nest,
    that flutters over its young,
spreading out its wings, catching them,
    bearing them on its pinions (Deuteronomy
32:11).

God is likened to a parent eagle with His eaglets. This
simile is a favorite of God's in His Word for His people,
who at this time lived near mountains and watched the
eagles high above raise eaglets in their nest to teach them
to fly and soar. Just like a parent eagle with us God does
three things. First, He stirs up our nest. Second, He hovers
over them. Thirdly, He spreads out His wings to swoop
down and catch us, bearing us up on His wings

First, He stirs up our nests. God is tender to make us a
nest, but also God is strong to stirs us out of it to learn to
fly. "Two things I know of You, O God, that You are
tender and You are strong" (NIV Psalm 81:7-8a). Parents,
especially mothers, are tender with their children in
building their nest for little ones to feel secure and grow
up. Parents, especially fathers, are strong to stir up the
nest, calling their little ones to leave home and take flight
in their callings.

Second, He hovers over us. As our children mature and begin to enter into the calling God has for their lives, He does not leave them alone for their first attempts at flying. He hovers over them. He wants them more dependent on Him than on the nest He made for them with their parents. In the same way parents participate with God in this process of hovering over their children.

Emily had learned to ride her bike, and we were going on a walk with her and her two little brothers. As Karen and I were buckling up the two boys in the stroller, Emily started down our driveway into the street where cars and trucks were driving by. When we realized she was headed for danger, Karen shouted "Bob!"

I ran towards Emily on her bike heading not only into the street but also across the street towards a ravine at the street's edge. She gracefully and happily went right in between a truck and a car, hit the curb, and began to soar in the air down into the ravine. It seemed like slow motion. I got there just on time to hover over her and to catch her in mid-flight. Do you know what she said after this amazing catch and rescue? "Daddy," she said, "can we do that again?" God was hovering over her, and He used her parents to spread out their wings in order to come swoop her up in the nick of time. God not only stirs up the nest, He hovers over children as they are learning to spread their wings and fly.

Thirdly, He spreads out His wings to swoop down and rescue us time and time again, bearing us up on His wings. In Exodus 19:4 God said: "You yourselves have seen what I did in Egypt, and how I carried you on eagles' wings and brought you to Myself." Just like a parent eagle with us God does three things: He stirs up our nest, He hovers over us, and He spreads out His wings to swoop down and catch us, bearing us up on His wings.

Jesus heavenly nest was stirred up. He took flight down to earth, even into the hands of sinful people. He spread out His "wings" on the cross to save us. After three days He rose from the dead to ascend and rise with healing in His wings. Then, He sent us on mission once more to the ends of the earth. Jesus' life of greatness is different from the good life we may expect for our children. What is the good life we are putting forth for our children when they leave the nest?

A Great Life is meant to Appear Ordinary

Sometimes we put forth too much in the way of expectations for our children because we misinterpret what greatness is – what it means to live the good life. The wisdom of Proverbs says: "Better to be ordinary and work for a living than act important and starve in the process" (Proverbs 12:9).

Long for greatness, dear Christian, but yield your definition of extraordinary to the one Jesus supplies. To begin with we must embrace this one important truth: "obscurity and greatness are not opposites."xxxv

Jesus is in the ordinary; He is of Nazareth. Place matters, even if it is small and somewhat despised. Jesus wants us to see the faces of the locals right under our noses. He said to His disciples (Luke 7:44): "Do you see this woman?" He saw Matthew at a tax table, a little man up a tree, and noticed the unnoticed in a crowd. Are we so focused on the "great" on our cell phones that we can't see the greatness of potential right under our noses?

Jesus seems to avoid fame, yet He was great. "Everyone is looking for you," His disciples declared as if He was in the wrong. He wasn't tweeting, blogging, or promoting His services. Jesus wasn't acting important and starving in the process. Do you possess stamina for going unnoticed by children, children in law, or your peers? Do you possess a spirituality to do a thousand unnoticed acts of kindness in a small place for God's glory?

Here is what the living take to heart at a funeral of a person, who lived a truly great life: that this funeral is about one who loved well and faithfully kept their vows day in and out; one who showed mercy by noticing the faces of the locals; and one who generously gave away their opportunities for fake greatness for the privilege of true greatness - loving well.

How does someone experience greatness? Great people realize on the front end that the Gospel is true for them personally. Let me put it this way: *you have already been discovered as the great and adorable person you are in Christ*, which frees you up to go discover others in the same light today. Proverbial wisdom from Solomon teaches us that it is better to be ordinary and work for a living than act important and starve trying to be someone else in the process. This is a vision for our children when we consider what it would mean for them to live a life of greatness in an age of celebrities.

How Parents Help Children Discover their Callings

God has a calling on everyone's life, and it is a parent's privilege to help a child discover a child's sense of this calling. How does a parent help in the discovery process? This can be done in three important ways by helping children discover and to live out of the hearts God gave them, by making the most of children's prevocational jobs, and by helping children own their longings.

Discovering the Heart God Gave Your Child

The passage usually cited as a guarantee to conscientious parents is: "Train up a child in the way he should go; even when he is old he shall not depart from it (Proverbs 22:6)." This truism is often viewed as a promise guaranteeing that if parents teach kids right from wrong until they are adults; they'll practice everything you taught them.

Actually, the proverb is not a promise; it is a truism describing a way of approaching life rather than prescribing a formula for promised results. This proverb invites parents into wisdom; namely, to discover a child's unique "bent," their inclination towards their callings. If parents work in concert with their children's uniqueness, the children won't depart from their God-given sense of calling when they are older. In order to discover the heart and inclination God gave a child towards calling, three questions may be asked from the prophet Micah's most famous words. The passage in Micah reads:

> He has showed you, O man, what is good. And what does the LORD require of you? To act justly and to love mercy and to walk humbly with your God (Micah 6:8).

This verse of scripture highlights three virtues that shall furnish parents for sensing their children's callings to Christ. We will ask the text three questions in a personal way in order to discover how it applies to one's sense of calling. The three virtues are justice, mercy, and humility. The three questions from these three virtues only you can answer.[xxxvi]

What Makes your Child Angry?

The first is justice. Act justly. Justice makes a Christian ask herself what makes me angry? There are injustices in our contemporary culture and oppression exists in our world that arouses a holy anger (Ephesians 4: 26) in our hearts. Which one makes your child slam his fist down and say, "No more!" Is it poverty? Is it economic injustice? Is it Internet theft? What makes you angry for justice? This righteous anger when constructively used in a slow manner for love's sake can energize your child to take action in the particular calling God is summoning him or her into.

One of the men I have investing my life into, I also led to Christ. He is married, and they have just adopted a boy from a far-away nation. I'll name him "Thankful

Beloved." If you asked this couple what makes them angry in a godly sense, you will see tears come down from their eyes as they tell you it is that there exist in this world too many unwanted children. They have a sense of calling to adopt the unwanted, and they have a very large family now of former orphans. This is what makes them long for justice. This is what makes them slow to anger.

The Gospel motivates them and brings them to surrender to the Father, who chose them in love out of the orphanage of a fallen world to be His beloved. The woman wrote me recently about her newly adopted son's unwillingness to surrender to his dad's will. She wrote something like this: "As I held this little boy in my arms and begged God to help my adopted son surrender, I also, in a sense, surrendered my own adopted heart to my heavenly Father." As was written above, children bring parents down to their knees in prayer and to the school of wisdom.

Righteous anger has to be embraced and can be used constructively and slowly to become a Christian who acts justly in one's calling to Christ, but calling also reflects a heart of mercy and compassion.

What Makes your Child Weep?

The second is mercy. "Love mercy." God's mercy is better than life. Jesus would often tell the self-righteous to go and ponder that God loves mercy more than our sacrifice. Mercy makes a Christian ask herself what makes me weep? Hannah wept for the privilege to have a child (1 Samuel 1: 10). As soon as Nehemiah heard the words about the brokenness in God's people he sat down and wept (Nehemiah 1: 4). Esther fell at her feet and wept for the evil Haman plotted to kill God's people, in a way like one would weep for the unborn and aborted today (Esther 8:3).

When the famous missionary to China, William C. Burns, was raised in a Christian home in Kilsyth, Scotland, his mother took him shopping in the big city of Glasgow. During the shopping trip William's mother lost his son in the crowds. When she finally found her son, who was a young teenager, she discovered him with tears streaming down his face. "Willie, my son, what ails you?" she asked with deep concern. William was struck by the sound of so many footsteps pounding on the pavement and wooden floors. William replied to his mother, "Oh, Mother! Mother! The thud of these Christless feet on their way to hell breaks my heart." This was a kairotic moment for William that shaped his sense of calling. William grew up, dressed and cut his hair like a Chinese teacher. He joined Hudson Taylor, each on a boat along a river, taking turns preaching to the Chinese along the banks of the river. When he died after a successful ministry of evangelism, a small box came back to his family containing all his belongings— a Bible and a spiritual journal.

William's mother asked her son, what makes you weep? This helped William discover God's call on his life to serve as an evangelist and a missionary. Although William had little in the way of possession and died young, he fulfilled his God-given calling by loving mercy. What makes your child angry? What makes your child weep? This is a way to discover the child's call to act justly and to love mercy, but the third virtue required of God is humility.

What Makes your Child Walk Humbly with God?

The third is humility. "Walk humbly with your God." Humility makes a Christian ask herself, What do I love to do? What makes you take steps? The Qoheleth said that there is nothing better than to find enjoyment in one's calling (Ecclesiastes 2: 24). The key is to walk to the end; to get started and to finish; to launch out and to depend on God until the end in a work one enjoys, and is good at, marked by humility.

Humility is what keeps one from getting stuck and being unwilling to risk and fulfill one's calling. In John Steinbeck's Cannery Row there is a character named Henri who never takes steps to fulfill his calling. Henri is a local artist and a friend of Doc's. No one is certain about Henri's artistic abilities, but everyone agrees he's doing a beautiful job building his boat. The boat has always been on locks in a vacant lot and has never been in the ocean. It is Henri's unfinished life work, however, because Henri is afraid of the ocean. Steinbeck wrote about a conversation between Hazel and Doc as they spoke about Henri's issues:

> Doc chuckled. "He still building his boat?"
> "Sure," said Hazel. "He's got it all changed
> around. New kind of a boat. I guess he'll take it
> apart and change it. Doc— is he nuts?" Doc
> swung his heavy sack of starfish to the ground and

stood panting a little. "Nuts?" he asked. "Oh, yes, I guess so. Nuts about the same amount we are, only in a different way." Such a thing had never occurred to Hazel. He looked upon himself as a crystal pool of clarity and on his life as a troubled glass of misunderstood virtue. Doc's last statement had outraged him a little. "But that boat—" he cried. "He's been building that boat for seven years that I know of. The blocks rotted out and he made concrete blocks. Every time he gets it nearly finished he changes it and starts over again. I think he's nuts. Seven years on a boat." Doc was sitting on the ground pulling off his rubber boots. "You don't understand," he said gently. "Henri loves boats but he's afraid of the ocean." "What's he want a boat for then?" Hazel demanded. "He likes boats," said Doc. "But suppose he finishes his boat. Once it's finished people will say, 'Why don't you put it in the water?' Then if he puts it in the water, he'll have to go out in it, and he hates the water. So you see, he never finishes the boat—so he doesn't ever have to launch it."[xxxvii]

We must walk humbly with God in our callings without refusing to finish what we began, and without fearing the completion. The humble know their weakness and attempt great things, even when fears of launch out are felt within.

What injustice in our culture arouses anger in your child when he or she sees evil score another victory? Where does your child's heart break with sorrow from what is still unredeemed? What brings a "yes" to your child's soul that makes him or her willing to offer their lives in humble service? Micah 6:8 can be useful for a child to discover an early sense of calling.

Parents differentiate their children from themselves to live out the calling God gave them. This process of launching children out begins when they are little by blessing them for a bright future, imitating God's likeness to a parent eagle, setting forth a life of greatness that may appear ordinary, and helping children discover the heart God gave them – a heart to act justly, love mercy, and walk humbly in a particular calling.

As children start out in the first jobs outside the home, it is helpful for them to see these first jobs as prevocational.

The Significance of Children's Prevocational Jobs

Even our difficult pre-vocations, which are temporary employments and first opportunities to work, are part of our overall calling to Christ. I worked in the steel mills of Gary, Indiana, during the summers while attending Purdue University for four years. I would leave my beautiful hometown of Ogden Dunes along Lake Michigan with sand dunes, beautiful woods, and beach life in order to drive into the polluted, productive steel mills to work. I wore a yellow helmet, protective goggles, special dark-green clothing, and steel-tipped boots. It was like serving for the armed forces in a war zone. I watched hot steel made from a liquid in furnaces where the workers wore metal-looking astronaut suits. The language was rough, and the culture was politically incorrect according to today's standards. They knew college students were temporary workers. It was my prevocational summer job that was important in my calling, but their vocational work mattered too.

They called us "summertime." "Hey, summertime," they'd call out to us, "dig this sludge out." We had the worst tasks imaginable at times, and we would say to each other, "I'm definitely finishing college so I never have to work here." When I drove out of the parking lot, there was a car-washing process to take off the falling soot from the cars. Before I showered at home, I used industrial soap to take the black grime from my hands. Although I did not see the job as my permanent calling, I learned to view it as an important step to discovering God's call on my life.

Now, what does that pre-vocational job of affliction have to do with my overall calling to Christ, and my particular calling to serve as a gospel preacher and senior pastor? Well, it was in the steel mills that I learned to respect people serving in jobs that others benefit from. It was there that someone first shared the gospel with me, though I wasn't ready to receive it. I learned about other cultures of all kinds that I had not known well until then. I came to appreciate all the trades that go into making steel, and I can trust that God was shaping my character and preparing me in the furnace of affliction for working even harder in the furnace of full-time vocational ministry.

God is behind our pre-vocations because he is behind our vocations. He puts on our heart our pre-vocations and avocations because they are on his heart too. Working jobs to get through schooling is an aspect of shaping us for a future vocation. Joseph served under his parents, a government official, and a prison guard before he served under the king as Egypt's "prime minister." David served as a shepherd to prepare him to serve as a warrior and a king to shepherd God's people. John, James, and Peter served as fishermen before they were fishers of men (Matthew 4: 19). Paul was a theological student and scholar, also a tent maker, before he was an apostle to the nations and a gospel theologian. Luke was a physician before and while he was serving as a missionary and sacred historian. We can trust that God purposefully designs every aspect of our overall general calling to Christ, and gives us particular callings that are often fashioned in the fields, prisons, boats, factories, and classrooms of affliction.

In fact, God has much to say to us in the bible about working, serving, and employment that it is a wonder how Christians made this major chunk of our lives seem so unimportant and "secular!" For, in the sight and presence of God throughout the week God is behind them in a sacred way. Just as the Greeks viewed manual labor as demeaning, Christendom in the medieval period viewed it as "secular" work, as less valuable to Christ than work in and for the Church. This is why Martin Luther attacked this false notion effectively in his treatise *To the Christian Nobility of the German Nation*:

> It is pure invention [fiction] that Pope, bishops, priests, and monks are called "spiritual estate" while princes, lords, artisans, and farmers are called the "temporal estate." This is indeed a piece of deceit and hypocrisy … Yet no one need be intimidated by it, and that for this reason: all

> Christians are truly of the spiritual estate, and
> there is no difference among them except that of
> office…We are all consecrated priests.[xxxviii]

The Reformers' understanding of how sacred and
important our work is to Christ ignited the laity to work as
to the Lord, rather than to please men (Colossians 3: 23–
24). By the twentieth century, however, many Protestant
churches were silent about this issue. In that period
Dorothy Sayers questioned why the Church was rarely
addressing how one's work matters to God, and why
preachers rarely use the Bible's many passages to do so.
In her essay, "Why Work?" in *Creed or Chaos* she
complains:

> The church's approach to an intelligent carpenter
> is usually confined to exhorting him to not be
> drunk and disorderly in his leisure hours and to
> come to church on Sundays. What the church
> should be telling him is this: that the very first
> demand that his religion makes upon him is that
> he should make good tables.[xxxix]

Parents differentiate their children from themselves to live
out the calling God gave them. This process of launching
children out begins when they are little by blessing them
for a bright future, imitating God's likeness to a parent
eagle, setting forth a life of greatness that may appear
ordinary, and helping children discover the heart God
gave them, and learning to appreciate prevocational
employment. Before we end this chapter, however, it is
important for parents to learn to draw out their children's
longings.

Discovering Your Child's Longings

When God took out our heart of stone, He put in a heart of flesh. He calls us to live out of the tender heart He gave us, which includes our longings. What do you long for? Longings and desires for knowing Christ, winning the lost, and loving people well are the fuel God gave us to move forward with tenderness and strength into our callings.

Counselor Larry Crabb helpfully describes three types of longings.[xl] These three types of longings are designated as our casual, critical, and crucial longings. First, there are casual longings for better circumstances and new provisions. Your casual longings may be for a clean house by the end of the day, a pay increase by year's end, or a good dinner tonight. Second, there are critical longings for deeper relationships and God's blessings for others. You may long for reconciliation with a family member, for a closer relationship to your spouse, or for a child to be saved. Third, there are crucial longings for God's unconditional love and for Himself. It is a longing to be satisfied in God and to walk closely with Him.

These three types of longings must be embraced, and not dismissed. To embrace them requires us to embrace the sorrow of unmet longings. Perhaps this was the reason why Jesus was called "a man of sorrows" (Isaiah 53; Hebrews 5: 7). Your children's longings tell them that they have glory; that they were built for God and a better day. The reason why nothing will ultimately satisfy us in this life is because we were made for glory and the new

earth. Creation, the Holy Spirit within us, and ourselves
all groan together until we experience the fullness and
satisfaction in God that we were created for (Romans 8:
18–30).

Longings are meant for our children to lean into the future
with hope. They fuel our children's callings. They cause
their deepest emotions to surface, which is one reason
why people are afraid of them. So often we are
embarrassed to cry in front of others when we express
them, but this is an illegitimate shame because these
tearful longings express our groans for our future glory.
Children in touch with their longings have a heart that is
present to Christ, people, and place.

Helping children discover their sense calling and place in
this world is an important process of parenting. It is
helpful for children and parents to discuss issues of social
justice, compassionate service, and what motivates them
to walk humbly with God in living out their giftedness in
life. It is also useful to make the most of prevocational
employment, and ask how God is preparing them for a
particular vocation in the future. Finally, children learn to
live out of the heart God gave in callings when they
embrace the longings God has placed on their hearts. In
the process of discovering callings children sense being
called to surrender and to sacrifice for the sake of loving
and serving others. They are learning to "take up their
cross" and to follow Christ to the place He will set them.

Children are likened to arrows in the quiver of parents
aiming their children out of the home and into the world
for Christ. Discovering and cultivating a sense of calling

to Christ in children sharpens these arrows to make an impact for Christ. In his remarkable classic, *Mere Christianity*, C. S. Lewis wrote something profound about our need to lose all – our self and possessions in order to receive it all back much better. He writes:

> [T]here must be a real giving up of the self. You must throw it away "blindly" so to speak. Christ will indeed give you a real personality: but you must not go to Him for the sake of that. As long as your own personality is what you are bothering about you are not going to Him at all. The very first step is to try to forget about the self altogether. Your real, new self (which is Christ's and also yours, and yours just because it is His) will not come as long as you are looking for it. It will come when you are looking at Him. Does that sound strange? . . . The principle runs through all life from top to bottom. Give up yourself, and you will find your real self. Lose your life and you will save it. Submit to death, death of your ambitions and favorite wishes every day and death of your whole body in the end: submit with every fiber of your being, and you will find eternal life. Keep back nothing. Nothing that you have not given away will ever be really yours. Nothing in you that has not died will ever be raised from the dead. Look for yourself, and you will find in the long run only hatred, loneliness, despair, rage, ruin, and decay. But look for Christ and you will find Him, and with Him everything else thrown in. Giving ourselves wholly to Christ is the only way

to discover who we are, the only way to become who Christ means us to be, the only way to experience his riches in this life and the only way to fulfill the purpose for which he made us. It may seem frightening, but once you do it, your only regret will be that you didn't do it sooner.[xli]

Lose your children for Jesus' sake and you will find them. Break any enmeshments with your children, while remaining involved in their lives. Children are "Isaacs" to be offered to God as Abraham offered his son, Isaac, upon the altar of sacrifice. George Whitefield, the famous evangelist of the Great Awakening, explains how sacrificing our children as Abraham did is ultimately the way God the Father offered His only Son for us. Whitefield wrote:

Some of you...may have children, in whose lives your own lives are bound up: all, I believe, have their Isaacs, their particular delights of some kind or other . . . resign them daily in affection to God, that, when He shall require you really to sacrifice them, you may not confer with flesh and blood, any more than [Abraham] . . . think, O think of the happiness he now enjoys, and how he in incessantly thanking God for tempting and trying him when here below...there I hope to sit with you, and hear the story of [the Father] offering up his Son from His own mouth, and to praise the Lamb that sits upon the throne, for what He has done for our souls, for ever and ever.[xlii]

This should be one of a parent's favorite areas of *raising children into Gospel maturity*, children learning how to discerning and fulfilling their callings with their parents help. This chapter showed the importance of seeing every calling as sacred, not just full-time vocational service as pastors or missionaries. The subjects related to this included the power of differentiated gender, pronouncing blessings over our children's heads, parenting like God as an eagle parent with eaglets, envisioning an ordinary life lived for Christ as greatness, cultivating justice, mercy and humility, giving significance to their prevocational jobs, and the discovery of longings. This process of parents engaged in discerning their children's callings will put them on the road to the place of calling where the disciple of Christ will engage in selfless mission for Christ. Children are launched like sharpened arrows aimed on making an impact for Christ in the world.

As children move out of the home and into their Father's world to the place He has for them, parents find themselves shifting gears in their role as parents. The next chapter looks at how parenting changes as children become like *willows by flowing streams*. It addresses how parents may become grandparents of children, who have reached Gospel maturity.

Discussion Questions

1. How do mothers and fathers play a vital role in gender differentiation? What is a mother's message to her children? What is a Gospel message from a father about a child's gender?

2. How have you spoken a good word about your child's future by way of a blessing or benediction? When is an appropriate time to do so?

3. How are parents and children like eagles teaching and learning how to soar and fly out of the nest?

4. Why is it important a great life as appearing somewhat ordinary? What are the dangers of hyper-spirituality when it involves expectations for our children?

5. How can parents help children to discover callings while still in the home?

6. Why is it important that a child live out of the heart God gave him or her?

7. What is your child's sense of justice? How does your child express his or her love for mercy in culture? What is your child's gifts and skills, which they love to do and can learn to humbly enjoy in life?

8. How can you help your child appreciate his or her prevocational jobs? What are ways God is preparing the child for a primary calling in the future?

9. What does your child long for casually, critically, and crucially?

Chapter Eight: Friendship and Grand Parenting

What may our future look like if we do *raise our children into Gospel maturity?* What if your children do become like *willows by flowing streams?* What comes next? "Empty nest" sounds sad to parents because there is actually such fullness in seeing children blossom. Parents need a long-term vision for parenting. This chapter discusses what it means for parents to cultivate friendships with their adult children *raised to Gospel maturity.*

It might encourage you to begin right away to pray for future spouses and to be open to a child's a call to be single for a long season or all of life. What follows in this chapter is a glance at what it looks like to walk your children through engagement to be married until their wedding day. It is a chapter about embracing children in law, and parenting in a new way; namely, the impact of grandparents on grandchildren. All this culminates for parents when they will leave a Gospel legacy from Christ to the next generation.

Parents of adult children soon find themselves in another season of parenting with new challenges and blessings. Common challenges include the sorrow an empty home or an empty nest, adult children living at home longer, delaying marriage, becoming friends, and getting engaged to be married.

Empty Nest

Oh my! When our last of five children had moved out after her wedding, Karen and I faced an empty nest for the first time. After James and Lizzy had a weeklong honeymoon, we helped load up their moving truck, cleaned out her empty room with an ache in our gut, and sat down on the sofa and wept. We couldn't talk. All we could do is cry. Our home was filled with children and their friends for over three decades. When we recovered, we asked: "Where did the time go?" Was the thirty-two years of parenting over? In one sense, it was. In another sense it was a denouement, only the end of a chapter, and the beginning of another season of parenting was on the horizon.

God fashioned our hearts according to the condition of His will, and we found ourselves quite content in about three months. The initial visits to our five married children and fourteen grandchildren, at first, brought tears to our eyes whenever we were heading back home. Over time, however, we have become used to the new normal in our lives. Every parent must consider that an empty nest will come after some twenty years of *raising a child into Gospel maturity*, but we still embrace the sorrow of unmet longings until heaven.

What is lifelike now? Karen and I enjoy every night sharing a meal, doing the dishes, and taking a walk. We have the whole house to ourselves until the children and grandchildren visit from time to time. Those visits are so much fun, and each empty room is filled with the five new families. The grandchildren run all over and play, and it is a taste of heaven.

Adult Children at Home

What if your child stays home for college or beyond? Actually, staying home during college is a great idea financially and spiritually, but beyond college American parents and children struggle over cultural expectations that these children ought to move out of the home by twenty-two years old. It will be much more enjoyable if parents and child are also friends, without enabling the adult child from leaving in a responsible fashion in the near future. Is it okay with you if your child does not sense a call to be married?

One of my treasures in the church I pastor is a daughter of a close friend, who would love for his daughter to be married. She is so godly and beautiful! She is a leader of women's bible study, and equipped in evangelism. I have been so impressed with her and her father because they both helped me witness and hear the biblical call to singleness. Maybe she will be married someday, but, for now, she is content and growing in the Lord. Paul advises this in 1 Corinthians 7. In the meantime, however, a mutual friendship can be cultivated.

Parents becoming Friends

One evening as we were standing in our front driveway, one of our children told us that hanging out with his siblings and us are more fun than hanging out with friends. Was that okay? I thought so, as long as we had no demands on them and encouraged them to cultivate friends and community. We have always enjoyed being with our children, and it has been mutual. We play games, talk about things we are doing or valuing, and worship together sometimes with guitar. We go on an annual vacation each year to Florida, and each family prepares a funny skit to perform.

The key for parents to become friends with their children is to spend time with them, and to restrain from telling them what to do. Rather, we can listen and learn from them, try out new music and clothing, and become interested in what they are interested in. They already know what you think because they listened to you for the most formative years of their lives. As children become adults sons grow facial hair, and sometimes they choose different styles of appearance than we would choose. The adult child, however, still asks the first same question all their lives; namely, "Do you love me?" The second question – can I have my own way – now, however, becomes a question they must learn to ask God the Father, and only seek advice from his or her parents.

One of the ways I still parent my adult children is through dates like when they were young, only now I include my sons and daughter-in-law. I take the sons out camping or to a ball game, and the daughters out to dinner or to shop for something special. We get to know each other because children are always changing. I remember my children as babies, at five, and in later years at ten, at sixteen, at twenty, etc., but I can always get to know them for who they have become now. We also watch their children so that they can go on dates as they did when they first met. Karen and I talk to them on the phone most days, and we have a family text and thread that is filled with videos, prayer requests, and praises.

Finding yourself in an empty nest with children gone, children living too long at home or remaining single longer than we expected, and learning to become friends with adult children are some of the new challenges parents face as the children become adults. Another new and foreign experience for a parent is watching your children become engaged and marry another.

When Your Children are engaged to be Married

Karen and I have been through this experience five times – three sons and two daughters. It is wonderfully fulfilling to see our years of praying answered; it is also frightening to give a daughter in marriage or to have a son leave for marriage to another woman. On the one hand, we gain a son or a daughter. On the other hand, we lose a son or a daughter. We increase through loss; we decrease through gain. It is what we always prayed for in a son or a daughter-in-law, but how come we feel loss or pain?

I will always remember when my son-in-law's ask for my two daughters' hands in marriage. It was predictable, and we were ready to answer in the affirmative. Tyson was the first man and Emily was our oldest. Tyson asked me on a man-to-man-time at *Potbellies* restaurant. After I said yes, he asked for a wedding in thirty days! She wasn't pregnant. They just desired a quick engagement. I said we have to pray, and that maybe Tyson and Emily could come to our home that night to talk.

When they came the next day, we had surrendered to saying yes. We realized that the only obstacle was our

effort to preserve our image before people, which was not
a good reason. After we granted them a short engagement,
I explained to Tyson that he might call me anything but
"Mr. Smart." Tyson asked, "Can I call you Dad?" I asked
why, and he replied: "I have never had a man I could call
'Dad.'" We both cried because it was what we both
longed for.

My three sons, on the other hand, each asked me for
advice and prayer for courage to ask their potential father-
in-law for their daughters hands in marriage. With each
son we walked and talked through how to simply ask the
big question: namely, "Mr. ____ may I please have your
daughter's hand in marriage?" I advised them after the
question to simply stop talking and to wait for the answer,
even if it seemed like eternity. Thankfully, each father
answered in the affirmative.

The Wedding Day

The movie, *Father of the Bride*, and other movies have
made it clear that weddings are expensive, fun, and
painful. Every time we have a wedding in our church, and
we have quite a few each year, a miracle of God takes
place when a father keeps his composure while walking
his daughter down the aisle without falling apart. It is a
transcendent experience when a father feels he has one
foot in the past and one foot in an unknown future. The
ceremony is a tearful, glorious blur for both mothers and
fathers when families unite as practical strangers for their
children's sake. This is fallowed up by a celebration,
which includes a father and mother's last dance with their
dear child. It is a joyful, fearful, and strangely good

celebration that costs a lot, but the parents would pay almost anything for their child's best of celebrations.

After the celebration there is cleanup and the tying up of loose ends. The two children go on a honeymoon together, and the parents of both children pray and wait. How wild is that?

What is it like to have a healthy relationship with a son or daughter married now to another daughter or son-in-law? One of my close friends said that he did not anticipate how much influence the spouse would have upon each of his children, as they were married. Parents lose the influence on they once enjoyed on their children, who were once single. Parents now share their children with other parents. Parenting at this stage is both a matter of losing influence and gaining trust in God for the adult child's future in marriage and family.

It is important to avoid enmeshment, especially between mother and daughter. The young couple needs time away from parents in order to establish their marriage as a separate unit from both sets of parents. Daughters are given, and a mother too involved with her daughter is a nightmare for the son-in-law and their future. Actually, it is a sign that the parent's marriage is unhealthy. A child-centered marriage may have taken hold years ago, but it is not a way of loving your children to continue this after the children are married.

Parents of adult children soon find themselves in another season of parenting with new challenges and blessings. Common challenges include the sorrow an empty home or an empty nest, adult children living at home longer, delaying marriage or remaining single, becoming friends, and getting engaged to be married. Sometime after marriage, however, there may be grandchildren, which is another stage of parenting.

Grandparents with New and Grand Children

Grandparents have a platform freely given to them by their children, and by virtue of being grandparents. It is a platform to influence the grandchildren for good or ill. A grandfather or grandmother hardly has to do anything to make an impact on his grandchildren. Grandpa is a hero, a legend, a star entertainer, and a personal confident from the get-go. Grandma is a walking candy machine, a favorite chef, a number one fan, and a personal counselor.

Becoming a grandparent happened fast for us, and was something to get used to because we felt so young. Our children married young, and they starting having children immediately. Our oldest two of fourteen grandchildren, Micaiah and Anna, both named us "Papa" and "Mema." These terms of endearment became our name for each of the grandchildren ever since. Now, children name us. When we have all the family over for a holiday like Christmas, we host about twenty-three people in our home. It is a delightful chaos, and the cousins love to play with each other. Soon we hope to leave a Gospel legacy to yet another generation.

Leaving a Gospel Legacy[xliii]

God gives a legacy as we live out a Gospel-centered life as parents. Your legacy answers the question: what's your life message? Ultimately, it is given in your final testament.

Your Final Testament

The testament has been an essential source for the study of the late Middle Ages and early modern period across a wide variety of disciplines, including legal history, property relations, linguistics, demography, women, marriage, the family, economy and material culture, and religious history, but especially in the study of popular piety, charity, burial choices, funerary practices, and the history of death and mentalities. This is because a testament is a written covenant of a Christian between himself or herself and God.

My great grandfathers and grandmothers left us written covenants they each made with God, which included promises for our family lineage. Your final testament can be one page and be included in your will. It is a written-out testimony or witness to God's greatness and grace to the Christian and God's promise to Christian's offspring. It may be recorded in an old family Bible or put in an envelope behind a family portrait. Paperless storage ideas are numerous for sustaining a testimony of God's grace to you in conversion and throughout your lifetime.

The Bible provides us with examples to encourage us that our final words are weighty. For example, Isaac's last words of grace to his twins pictured a bright future for them and even the end of their fighting with one another (Genesis 27: 27– 29, 39– 40). Jacob, or Israel, spoke beautiful words to his son Joseph and his grandsons Ephraim and Manasseh (Genesis 48: 15– 22). The twelve sons of Israel receive a final word, which was prophetic and pointed to Christ's coming (Genesis 49: 1– 28).

We have examples in the New Testament too. Simeon and Anna were in the final season of spiritual formation. They each have a legacy from Christ and speak a final life message. Anna was advanced in years and a widow for most of her life. She devoted her life to the word and to prayer night and day, looking forward to the coming of Christ. Her last message is recorded in Luke's gospel. Luke says, "She began to give thanks to God and to speak of him to all who were waiting for the redemption of Jerusalem" (Luke 2: 38).

Simeon, too, had a final word concerning Christ. Simeon was in the Spirit when he took up in his arms the baby Jesus, whom he had waited his life to see with his own eyes. Simeon thanked God that now he could depart in peace, according to a word from God. It was a message for Mary and Joseph about Christ, their child, as the light of the nations and glory of Israel. Simeon's final word caused Mary and Joseph to marvel at what was said of Jesus (Luke 2: 27– 33). Final words matter, especially when they are backed up by a whole life of Christian experience.

What is your legacy going to be? Well, in a way it is the Gospel message lived out in your children when they become *willows by flowing streams*. When your children are where you were, perhaps if they are parents. When they are *raising their children into Gospel maturity* with the same Gospel message.

Children are still listening to their parents' life message as they watch their parents die in a way that says, "Heaven is gain." Dying well takes place when living is Christ.

During the last minutes of his life, his thoughts and words were for his beloved wife Sarah. He whispered to one of his daughters, Lucy:

> It seems to me to be the will of God, that I must shortly leave you; therefore give my kindest love to my dear wife, and tell her, that the uncommon union, which has so long subsisted between us, has been of such a nature, as I trust is spiritual, and therefore will continue forever: and I hope she will be supported under so great a trial, and submit cheerfully to the will of God.[xliv]

A week and a half later Sarah wrote to Esther (it had been only six months since Esther's husband had died):

> My very dear child, What shall I say? A holy and good God has covered us with a dark cloud. O that we may kiss the rod, and lay our hands upon our mouths! The Lord has done it. He has made me adore his goodness, that we had him so long. But my God lives; and he has my heart. O what a legacy my husband, and your father, has left us! We are all given to God; and there I am, and love to be. Your affectionate mother, Sarah Edwards.[xlv]

So, begin now the things that matter then. Do this in the everyday way of living out the Gospel in what may appear ordinary to many, but will become weighty in the end.

Discussion Questions

1. What do you feel about being in "an empty nest?" What are the pros and cons?

2. Do you have an adult child at home still? How can you help your child learn to be single as a calling? What are ways that you parent more to empower and not to enable?

3. What does it look like to become friends with your children? What do friends do together? How can you cultivate more friendship with your child?

4. How does your child's engagement to be married make you feel? What do you fear? What is a Gospel message that would help your child prepare for marriage? Is your child willing to receive premarital counseling from a trusted pastor?

5. How can you prepare your child and your own heart for a wedding day? What are common stresses in wedding planning that you may preclude with God's help and wisdom?

6. What are two ways a grandparent can make a difference in a grandchild's life? How is the role of a grandparent different from that of a parent?

7. What legacy are you aiming for now? What do you need to begin now that will matter most in the end?

Conclusion: A Vision Realized

God loves to give Christian parents vivid pictures of our children's future; of when they are *raised into Gospel maturity*, and these similes and metaphors motivate us how to parent towards a beautiful end. One of these similes to help parents envision adult children is of *willow trees by streams of living water* (Isaiah 44:2-5). Children, like willows, require the flowing streams of living water, the Holy Spirit, to grow into maturity and fruitfulness, which God promises. Something outside of Gospel parenting is required; namely, the Holy Spirit.

God put forth this promise in Isaiah 44:3-5 that He will pour out the Holy Spirit into the thirsty lives of children – children of promise. God has always had it on His heart from all eternity to glorify His Son in the outpourings of His Spirit upon all flesh, but particularly on believers' children's children. "I will pour out My Spirit on your offspring."

On the day when Christ ascended, the Father gave Him the Spirit of Promise, and He poured out the Spirit in great measure. On that day of Pentecost Peter said, "the promise is for you, your children, and for all who are far off" (Acts 2). The promise repeated in the Old and New Testaments if for the children whose parents call on the Name of the Lord for salvation.

We, as parents, are seeking God's Spirit to be poured out upon our children of promise that they may be born again and filled with a divine sense of His presence and calling. Let us consider together what it means to *raise them into*

Gospel maturity and become like *willows by flowing streams*.

To this end, then, chapter one addressed the need for parents or a single parent to stay warmly present with a unified vision for their children like the triune God. They must learn and teach how to embrace the sorrow of unmet longing that every image bearer has in relationships. Fundamentally, the parents are called to establish a solid sense of Identity in Christ and engage in spiritual warfare against the lies of the evil one.

Chapter two explained the implications of what it means that children are gifts from God, which fuels parents with gratitude for the children God gives them. Sometimes that means being thankful for a special needs child. It emphasized how to dedicate children to the Lord, the significance of naming children, and what it may look like to trust God's promises on their behalf. This leads to the posture of parenting; namely, chapter three.

In chapter three parents are somewhat raised by their children as God brings parents to their knees, to silence before God, to Gospel repentance, and to the school of wisdom.

Chapter four shed biblical light on the nature of discipline. There are right and wrong ways to practice disciplining children, and it considered the four ways children tend to approach their parents. This chapter identified the two primary questions children are asking their parents, different forms of discipline, the three weightiest character qualities to emphasize, and how to keep the bridge when children are unrepentant for a season.

Chapter five applied Deuteronomy chapter six and is entitled life on life, missional discipleship. It considered various forms areas of education, teaching the Gospel and theology. It addressed such subjects as sanctification, sexuality, and maturity, which lead naturally to worship – chapter six.

In chapter six explained how parents mark their children's view and love of God, and therefore how they express their affections for God in song, prayer, education, and work in the home, church, and with their possessions and global concern that all the peoples of the earth give God glory.

One of my favorite chapters was chapter seven, which is about children learning to discern and fulfill their God-given callings with their parents help. It showed the importance of seeing every calling as sacred, not just full-time vocational service as pastors or missionaries. It answered and put forth a vision for the good life, which is an ordinary and weighty one lived under God's smile. This chapter contained subjects like promoting differentiated leadership, cultivating compassionate service, redeeming prevocational jobs, and engaging in missions.

Finally, this book ended with a chapter about a long-term vision for parenting. Chapter eight discussed what it means to cultivate friendships with adult children raised to Gospel maturity. It was a chapter for parents to begin now praying for future spouses or a call to singlehood, walking children through engagement to their wedding days, embracing children in law, and parenting in a new way; namely, the impact of grandparents on grandchildren. All this culminated for parents to leave a legacy from Christ to the next generation.

On a personal note, Karen and I are always learning about what it means for believing parents to *raise children into Gospel maturity*. Although our children and children in law are like *willows by flowing streams*, we must trust God's promise once more for the next generation. By God's grace alone our children and children in law are filled with the Spirit, they are all married, and are parents of our fourteen grandchildren. We love and pray for many wonderful parents still waiting on God's promise to pour out His Spirit on their children. We have lived this book, and we share a burden for you as parents, who are taking time to read and apply God's wisdom to do the same.

May the God of hope fill you with all joy and peace in believing, so that by the power of the Holy Spirit you may abound in hope as you read each chapter and apply it to your parenting and dear children of promise.

Putting it Down in Writing

Please consider taking time to fill out the following template in order to share with a support group aimed to strengthen parenting in your lives.

Template for Parent(s) to Raise Children into Gospel Maturity

God has called us/me to raise the children He gave us/me into Gospel maturity. To this end we/I am have great hope for _____ (children's _____ names)

_____

_____

_____ to become one day like *willows by flowing streams* as Isaiah 44:3-5 promises.

This begins with inviting and enjoying the presence of God in our home – the Father, the Son, and the Holy Spirit. His unified presence is what makes us feel secure, and so I am going to stay warmly present to my children and embrace the sorrow when my longings are unmet. I will not be ruled by anxiety, fear, and conflict, which often shows up when

_____

_____

_____

_____.

I renounce my parent's wrong family messages that said

_____

_____ and take captive and renounce the lie that I

_____

_____.

Lie that ___, but I will act out of who I am as a parent – accepted as righteous in God's sight, pardoned of all my sins, chosen in love to be God's beloved child, and set apart as a saint for holy living. This frees me up to help establish my children's solid sense of identity in Christ.

My son, _____, is glorious in his masculinity in the following ways _____

_____. My son is fallen in his masculinity and feels the Genesis 3 curse of inadequacy in the following ways ____

_____, and therefore a "glorious ruin." My role as a parent is to help him realize that the curse was meant to bring him to Christ. I will help him admit that he is licked, and that he must cry out for Christ to be his strength in his weakness. I will instruct him to consider and to live out what it looks like to be a redeemed son and man someday.

My daughter, _____, is glorious in her femininity in the following ways _____

_____. My Daughter is fallen in her femininity and feels the Genesis 3 curse of loneliness in the following ways

_____, and therefore a "glorious ruin." My role as a parent is to help her realize that the curse was meant to bring her to Christ. I will help her admit that she is licked, her controlling of relationships won't work, and that she must cry out for Christ to satisfy her longings for intimacy. I will instruct her to consider and to live out what it looks like to be a redeemed daughter and woman someday.

I will engage in spiritual warfare against Satan's lies and condemning thoughts aimed at my children and help my son and my daughter renounce the central condemning thought in his heart that he or she is

_____

_____ and his foolish strategies of

_____ to

prove what is not necessary in light of the Gospel.

_____ (name(s) of children are children of promise. My child was purposefully given to me by God, who is sovereign, to raise him or her to Gospel maturity. Therefore, I will pray the promises of scripture such as Isaiah 44:3-5 and others

_____.

I thank God for _____ (child's name), whose name means _____

_____. I dedicated

_____ (child's name) to the Lord and will trust God for his or her salvation.

The posture of my parenting is one of grace. God gave my children me as their parent, and God is raising me into Gospel maturity by bringing me to my knees when

_____, bringing me to
be silent before God when _____
_____, bringing me to
repentance when _____,
and bringing me to the school of wisdom by
_____.

My son _____ and my daughter _____ ask
me the two primary questions in one way or another to
see if they are loved and if they can have their own way. I
am learning how to answer these two questions by
_____.

My child _____ moves *towards* me as a *compliant*
child;
My child _____ moves *against* me as an *aggressive*
child;
My child _____ moves *away* from me as a
perfectionist child.

I am giving pause to the wrong ways I discipline my
children, which has been _____
_____,
and I am committed to seeing discipline times as
awesome opportunities to pour wisdom into my children.
Some of the ways I could do this better is by
_____
_____.

I am committed to major on the majors, and shape my
children over what really matters – Justice motivated by
love, mercy in conflicts, and faithfulness in the little
things – which means I must improve in the following
ways _____

_____.

I am teaching my children to learn to play second fiddle
and   to   build   others   up   by
_____
_____
_____.

My child _____ (name) has been challenging
of lately and we are committed to keeping the bridge by
_____
_____.

As a result of the mandate to disciple my children and in
light of Deuteronomy 6, I am going to consider creative
ways to do so while sitting in our home, walking on our
way, going to bed, and rising up in the morning. These
include _____

_____
_____.

I am planning to take my child _____ on a
date to _____ and I am committed to listen

before speaking to quickly, but I am praying for
_____.

I am teaching each child the cost of discipleship and to lose oneself for Jesus' sake in order to find oneself with a new identity in Christ.

When it comes to leading our children in worship in all of life, I could improve by
_____. I want to gather for a time of prayer as a family and learn to worship together by _____.

In order to promote differentiation of each child in order that each may hear God's voice and calling for them to leave and live a good life, I am committed to giving my child a blessing every night before bed. This is beneficial for my children because _
_____. I am willing to parent like God, who compares Himself to a parent eagle with eaglets stirred out of the nest for flying lessons. I could grow in this by
_____.

My child _____ (name) has a righteous anger for social justice in _____.
My child _____ (name) has a compassionate heart and weeps for _____.
My child _____ (name) is humbly gifted in and loves to _____.

My child _____ (name) has a prevocational job doing _____ and I am helping him or her see God's purposes in it.

My child _____ (name) longs for _____.
My child _____ (name) is afraid of longings, but I am helping him or her own them to discover the heart God gave them.

I am preparing for an empty nest by _____. I am not enabling my adult child to live at home as long as I _____ and he or she ___ _____.

I am preparing for, in the process of, my children's engagements to be married and we talk about it because _____.

What will your child's wedding day be like? What was it like for you as a parent of a married child? I will not enmesh with my child, which means _____ _____.

Grandparents have a platform to shape future generations; therefore I plan to live in an intentional way towards my children   and   grandchildren   by

_____

_____.

In all this I seek to leave a Gospel legacy as a parent, who *raised children into Gospel maturity* and impacted future generations as a grandparent for Christ so that they become like *willows by flowing streams*.

Appendix: Scriptural References on Parenting

Genesis 17:18
And Abraham said to God, "Oh that Ishmael might live
before you!"

Genesis 18:19
For I have chosen him, that he may command his
children and his household after him to keep the way of
the Lord by doing righteousness and justice, so that the
Lord may bring to Abraham what he has promised him."

Genesis 48:9
"They are the sons God has given me here," Joseph said
to his father. Then Israel said, "Bring them to me so I may
bless them."

Genesis 48:15
And he blessed Joseph and said, "The God before whom
my fathers Abraham and Isaac walked, the God who has
been my shepherd all my life long to this day,

Exodus 20:5
You shall not bow down to them or serve them, for I the
Lord your God am a jealous God, visiting the iniquity of
the fathers on the children to the third and the fourth
generation of those who hate me,

Exodus 20:12
"Honor your father and your mother, that your days may
be long in the land that the Lord your God is giving you.

Exodus 21:15
"Whoever strikes his father or his mother shall be put to death.

Leviticus 19:3
Every one of you shall revere his mother and his father, and you shall keep my Sabbaths: I am the Lord your God.

Exodus 10:2
And that you may tell in the hearing of your son and of your grandson how I have dealt harshly with the Egyptians and what signs I have done among them, that you may know that I am the Lord."

Deuteronomy 4:9
"Only take care, and keep your soul diligently, lest you forget the things that your eyes have seen, and lest they depart from your heart all the days of your life. Make them known to your children and your children's children—

Deuteronomy 5:16
"'Honor your father and your mother, as the Lord your God commanded you, that your days may be long, and that it may go well with you in the land that the Lord your God is giving you.

Deuteronomy 6:6-9
And these words that I command you today shall be on your heart. You shall teach them diligently to your children, and shall talk of them when you sit in your

house, and when you walk by the way, and when you lie down, and when you rise. You shall bind them as a sign on your hand, and they shall be as frontlets between your eyes. You shall write them on the doorposts of your house and on your gates.

Deuteronomy 11:19
You shall teach them to your children, talking of them when you are sitting in your house, and when you are walking by the way, and when you lie down, and when you rise.

Deuteronomy 21:18-21
"If a man has a stubborn and rebellious son who will not obey the voice of his father or the voice of his mother, and, though they discipline him, will not listen to them, then his father and his mother shall take hold of him and bring him out to the elders of his city at the gate of the place where he lives, and they shall say to the elders of his city, 'This our son is stubborn and rebellious; he will not obey our voice; he is a glutton and a drunkard.' Then all the men of the city shall stone him to death with stones. So you shall purge the evil from your midst, and all Israel shall hear, and fear.

Joshua 4:20-24
And those twelve stones, which they took out of the Jordan, Joshua set up at Gilgal. And he said to the people of Israel, "When your children ask their fathers in times to come, 'What do these stones mean?' then you shall let your children know, 'Israel passed over this Jordan on dry ground.' For the Lord your God dried up the waters of

the Jordan for you until you passed over, as the Lord your God did to the Red Sea, which he dried up for us until we passed over, so that all the peoples of the earth may know that the hand of the Lord is mighty, that you may fear the Lord your God forever."

Judges 2:10
And all that generation also were gathered to their fathers. And there arose another generation after them who did not know the LORD or the work that he had done for Israel.

1 Samuel 3:13
And I declare to him that I am about to punish his house forever, for the iniquity that he knew, because his sons were blaspheming God, and he did not restrain them.

2 Samuel 12:16
David therefore sought God on behalf of the child. And David fasted and went in and lay all night on the ground.

Psalm 37:25
I was young and now I am old, yet I have never seen the righteous forsaken or their children begging bread.

Psalm 78:4
We will not hide them from their children, but tell to the coming generation the glorious deeds of the Lord, and his might, and the wonders that he has done.

Psalm 103:13
As a father shows compassion to his children, so the Lord
shows compassion to those who fear him.

Psalm 103:17
But from everlasting to everlasting the LORD's love is
with those who fear him, and his righteousness with their
children's children—

Psalm 127:3-5
Behold, children are a heritage from the Lord, the fruit of
the womb a reward. Like arrows in the hand of a warrior
are the children of one's youth. Blessed is the man who
fills his quiver with them! He shall not be put to shame
when he speaks with his enemies in the gate.

Proverbs 1:8-9
Hear, my son, your father's instruction, and forsake not
your mother's teaching, for they are a graceful garland
for your head and pendants for your neck.

Proverbs 3:11-12
My son, do not despise the Lord's discipline or be weary
of his reproof, for the Lord reproves him whom he loves,
as a father the son in whom he delights.

Proverbs 10:1
A wise son makes a glad father, but a foolish son is a
sorrow to his mother.

Proverbs 13:18
Poverty and disgrace come to him who ignores instruction, but whoever heeds reproof is honored.

Proverbs 13:24
Whoever spares the rod hates his son, but he who loves him is diligent to discipline him.

Proverbs 17:6
Children's children are a crown to the aged, and parents are the pride of their children.

Proverbs 19:18-19
Discipline your son, for there is hope; do not set your heart on putting him to death. A man of great wrath will pay the penalty, for if you deliver him, you will only have to do it again.

Proverbs 22:6
Train up a child in the way he should go; even when he is old he will not depart from it.

Proverbs 22:15
Folly is bound up in the heart of a child, but the rod of discipline drives it far from him.

Proverbs 23:13
Do not withhold discipline from a child; if you strike him with a rod, he will not die.

Proverbs 23:22

Listen to your father who gave you life, and do not despise your mother when she is old.

Proverbs 23:24
The father of the righteous will greatly rejoice; he who fathers a wise son will be glad in him.

Proverbs 29:17
Discipline your son, and he will give you rest; he will give delight to your heart.

Proverbs 29:15
The rod and reproof give wisdom, but a child left to himself brings shame to his mother.

Isaiah 38:19
The living, the living, he thanks you, as I do this day; the father makes known to the children your faithfulness.

Isaiah 44:3-5
For I will pour water on the thirsty land,
    and streams on the dry ground;
I will pour my Spirit upon your offspring,
    and my blessing on your descendants.
They shall spring up among the grass
    like willows by flowing streams.
This one will say, "I am the LORD's,"
    another will call on the name of Jacob,
and another will write on his hand, "The LORD's,"
    and name himself by the name of Israel.

Isaiah 46:4-5
Even to your old age and gray hairs I am he, I am he who will sustain you. I have made you and I will carry you; I will sustain you and I will rescue you. 5 "With whom will you compare me or count me equal? To whom will you liken me that we may be compared?

Isaiah 65:23
They shall not labor in vain or bear children for calamity, for they shall be the offspring of the blessed of the Lord, and their descendants with them.

Malachi 4:6
And he will turn the hearts of fathers to their children and the hearts of children to their fathers, lest I come and strike the land with a decree of utter destruction."

Joel 1:3
Tell your children of it, and let your children tell their children, and their children to another generation.

Matthew 18:6
But whoever causes one of these little ones who believe in me to sin, it would be better for him to have a great millstone fastened around his neck and to be drowned in the depth of the sea.

Matthew 18:1-35
At that time the disciples came to Jesus, saying, "Who is the greatest in the kingdom of heaven?" And calling to him a child, he put him in the midst of them and said, "Truly, I say to you, unless you turn and become like

children, you will never enter the kingdom of heaven. Whoever humbles himself like this child is the greatest in the kingdom of heaven. Whoever receives one such child in my name receives me

Matthew 18:10
"See that you do not despise one of these little ones. For I tell you that in heaven their angels always see the face of my Father who is in heaven.

Matthew 19:13-14
Then children were brought to him that he might lay his hands on them and pray. The disciples rebuked the people, but Jesus said, "Let the little children come to me and do not hinder them, for to such belongs the kingdom of heaven."

Mark 5:23
And implored him earnestly, saying, "My little daughter is at the point of death. Come and lay your hands on her, so that she may be made well and live."

Mark 9:42
Whoever causes one of these little ones who believe in me to sin, it would be better for him if a great millstone were hung around his neck and he were thrown into the sea.

Luke 1:17
And he will go before him in the spirit and power of Elijah, to turn the hearts of the fathers to the children, and

the disobedient to the wisdom of the just, to make ready for the Lord a people prepared."

Luke 15:11-32
And he said, "There was a man who had two sons. And the younger of them said to his father, 'Father, give me the share of property that is coming to me.' And he divided his property between them. Not many days later, the younger son gathered all he had and took a journey into a far country, and there he squandered his property in reckless living. And when he had spent everything, a severe famine arose in that country, and he began to be in need. So he went and hired himself out to one of the citizens of that country, who sent him into his fields to feed pigs. ...

Acts 2:38-39
And Peter said to them, "Repent and be baptized every one of you in the name of Jesus Christ for the forgiveness of your sins, and you will receive the gift of the Holy Spirit. For the promise is for you and for your children and for all who are far off, everyone whom the Lord our God calls to himself."

2 Corinthians 12:14
Here for the third time I am ready to come to you. And I will not be a burden, for I seek not what is yours but you. For children are not obligated to save up for their parents, but parents for their children.

Ephesians 6:1-3
Children, obey your parents in the Lord, for this is right. "Honor your father and mother" (this is the first commandment with a promise), "that it may go well with you and that you may live long in the land."

Colossians 3:20-21
Children, obey your parents in everything, for this pleases the Lord. Fathers, do not provoke your children, lest they become discouraged.

Titus 1:6
If anyone is above reproach, the husband of one wife, and his children are believers and not open to the charge of debauchery or insubordination.

Titus 2:4
And so train the young women to love their husbands and children,

Titus 2:7
Show yourself in all respects to be a model of good works, and in your teaching show integrity, dignity,

2 Timothy 1:5
I am reminded of your sincere faith, which first lived in your grandmother Lois and in your mother Eunice and, I am persuaded, now lives in you also.

2 Timothy 3:2

For people will be lovers of self, lovers of money, proud, arrogant, abusive, disobedient to their parents, ungrateful, unholy,

2 Timothy 3:14-15

But as for you, continue in what you have learned and have become convinced of, because you know those from whom you learned it, and how from infancy you have known the Holy Scriptures, which are able to make you wise for salvation through faith in Christ Jesus.

2 Timothy 3:16-17

All Scripture is breathed out by God and profitable for teaching, for reproof, for correction, and for training in righteousness, that the man of God may be competent, equipped for every good work.

Titus 2:1-5

You, however, must teach what is appropriate to sound doctrine. Teach the older men to be temperate, worthy of respect, self-controlled, and sound in faith, in love and in endurance. Likewise, teach the older women to be reverent in the way they live, not to be slanderers or addicted too much wine, but to teach what is good. Then they can urge the younger women to love their husbands and children, to be self-controlled and pure, to be busy at home, to be kind, and to be subject to their husbands, so that no one will malign the word of God.

Hebrews 11:20
By faith Isaac invoked future blessings on Jacob and Esau.

Hebrews 12:5-11
And have you forgotten the exhortation that addresses you as sons? "My son, do not regard lightly the discipline of the Lord, nor be weary when reproved by him. For the Lord disciplines the one he loves, and chastises every son whom he receives." It is for discipline that you have to endure. God is treating you as sons. For what son is there whom his father does not discipline? If you are left without discipline, in which all have participated, then you are illegitimate children and not sons. Besides this, we have had earthly fathers who disciplined us and we respected them. Shall we not much more be subject to the Father of spirits and live? ...

1 Peter 5:5-6
Likewise, you who are younger, be subject to the elders. Clothe yourselves, all of you, with humility toward one another, for "God opposes the proud but gives grace to the humble." Humble yourselves, therefore, under the mighty hand of God so that at the proper time he may exalt you,

Endnotes

[i] Scripture quotations are from the ESV ® Bible (The Holy Bible, English Standard Version) (Crossway, 2001). Used by permission. All rights reserved. Other translations are marked accordingly.

[ii] While wild olives are propagated from seeds, cultivated olives are planted using shoots that grow at the base of another olive tree. Psalm 128:3 uses this imagery in comparing children to olive shoots around the table, and describes a godly mother as a fruitful vine within her house with her children as olive shoots around her at the family dinner table.

[iii] This is a theological term for the joy and self-less love between the Persons of the Godhead. Timothy Keller wrote: "The life of the Trinity is characterized not by self-centeredness but by mutually self-giving love. When we delight and serve someone else, we enter into a dynamic orbit around him or her, we center on the interests and desires of the other. That creates a dance, particularly if there are three persons, each of whom moves around the other two." *The Reason for God: Belief in an Age of Skepticism* (Grand Rapids, MI: Zondervan, 2010), pp. 214-215.

[iv] Bernard of Clairvaux, *Sermon 8 on Song of Songs.*

[v] Gregory of Nazianzus, *Oratio* 41, *Patrologia Graeca,* ed. by J.P. Migne (Paris, 1857-1866), pp. 36, 417.

[vi] Jonathan Edwards, "The Miscellanies," a-500, ed. Thomas A. Schafer, *The Works of Jonathan Edwards,* (New Haven: Yale University Press, 1994), vol. 13, p. 328.

[vii] John Calvin, *Institutes of the Christian Religion,* Book I, Chapter 13, Section 2.

viii Jonathan Edwards, _The Works of Jonathan Edwards_ (New Haven,
CT: Yale University Press, 1999), Vol. 17, pp. 437-438.

ix See Paul's prayer in Ephesians 3:14-21.

x Edith Schaeffer, _What is A Family?_ (Grand Rapids, MI: Baker Book
House, 1975), p. 27.

xi Leon Howard, _Herman Melville: A Biography_ (Berkley and Los
Angelos, CA: University of California Press, 1952), p. 137.

xii Paul David Tripp, _Parenting: 14 Gospel Principles That Can
Radically Change Your Family_ (Wheaton, IL: Crossway, 2016), p.
71.

xiii Satan has a twofold strategy in general. He tempts us when we are
proud to transgress and accuses Christians when prone to self-
condemnation. See Thomas Brooks, _Precious Remedies Against
Satan's Devices_ (Edinburgh, Scotland: reprinted, 1968), chapter one.

xiv See Beth McCord's helpful blog, _The Enneagram Coach:_
www.yourenneagramcoach.com

xv Robert Davis Smart, _Embracing Your Identity in Christ: Renouncing
Lies and Foolish Strategies_ (Bloomington, IN: WestBow, 2017).

xvi Carol Gilligan offers insights on this and concludes: "Since
masculinity is defined through separation while femininity is defined
through attachment, male gender identity is threatened by intimacy
while female gender identity is threatened by separation." Carol
Gilligan, _In a Different Voice_ (Cambridge, Mass.: Harvard University
Press, 1982), p. 173.

xvii C. S. Lewis, Prince Caspian (New York: HarperTrophy, 1951), p.
218.

xviii Dr. James Dobson, _Bringing Up Boys_, (Wheaton, IL: Tyndale
House Publishers, Inc., 2001), p.4

xix Thomas Brooks, _Precious Remedies Against Satan's Devices_
(Edinburgh, Scotland: reprinted, 1968), pp. 9-10.

xx Dan B. Allender, _How Children Raise Parents_ (Colorado Springs, CO:
Waterbrook Press, 2003), pp. 24-27.

xxi These three categories of children are based on Dr. Karen
Horney's theory of emotional disorder. I have made use of her
observations of pathology in children and parenting from the
biblical assumption that children are bent on autonomy and
depravity in need of God's grace.

xxii http:// www.hstuac.org/ muncyjim.html; https:// www.huntington.edu/ news/ dobson-to-graduates-be-there

xxiii "Education without values, as useful as it is, seems rather to make man a more clever devil."

xxiv Kairos in the Greek New Testament means a significant moment outside of ordinary time (chronos), which is pregnant with opportunity for furthering the kingdom of God.

xxv Ameriprise Study, http://newsroom.ameriprise.com/images/20018/RetirementDerailersResearchReport.pdf

xxvi Concordia Publishing has a "Learning About Sex Series," see Books 1-6. For example, Ruth Hummel, *Where Do Babies Come From? For Ages 6 to 8 and Parents* (Saint Louis, MO: Concordia Publishing House, 1995)

xxvii C. S. Lewis, *The Four Loves*, (London and Glasgow: Fontana Books, 1963), pp. 48-50, 54.

xxviii C. S. Lewis, *The Abolition of Man*, p. 101.

xxix C. S. Lewis, *Mere Christianity*, (1952; Harper Collins: 2001) 196-198.

xxx Corrie Ten Boom with John and Elizabeth Sherrill, *The Hiding Place: The Triumphant True Story of Corrie Ten Boom* (New York, NY: Bantam Books, 1974), pp. 39-41.

xxxi For a beautiful call to live in the ordinary way as a Christian, see Zack Eswine, *Sensing Jesus: Life and Ministry as a Human Being* (Wheaton, IL: Crossway, 2013).

xxxii Tripp, Paul David, *Parenting: 14 Gospel Principles That Can Radically Change Your Family* (Wheaton, IL: Crossway, 2016), pp. 152-153.

xxxiii Robert Davis Smart, *Legacy from Christ: What's My Message?* (Bloomington, IN: Westbow Press, 2017), pp. 31-33.

xxxiv John C. Paton. *John C. Paton: Missionary to the New Hebredes, an Autobiography Edited by His Brother*. Edinburgh: The Banner of Truth Trust, 1965, orig. 1889, 1891, 25– 26.

xxxv See Zack Eswine, *The Imperfect Pastor: Discovering Joy in Our Limitations through a Daily Apprenticeship with Jesus* (Wheaton, IL: Crossway, 2015).

xxxvi This section is taken from my book on calling. Robert Davis Smart, *Calling to Christ: Where's My Place?* (Bloomington, IN: Westbow Press, 2017) xxxvii Steinbeck, John. *Cannery Row* (Penguin Publishing Group. Kindle Edition), Kindle Locations 440-448.

xxxviii Martin Luther, *Three Treatises* (Philadelphia, PA: Fortress Press, 1970), p. 12.

xxxix Robert Davis Smart. *Calling to Christ: Where's My Place?* (pp. 22-23).

xl Larry Crabb, *InsideOut* (Colorado Springs, CO: Navpress, 1988), pp. 80-85.

xli C. S. Lewis, *Mere Christianity* (New York: Touchstone, 1996), pp 190-191.

xlii George Whitefield, *Fifteen sermons preached on various important subjects, by George Whitefield, A.B. late of Pembroke College, Oxford. ; Carefully corrected and revised according to the best London edition; To which is prefixed, a sermon, on the character, preaching, &c. of the Rev. Mr. Whitefield. By Joseph [i.e., Josiah] Smith, V.D.M.* (Philadelphia: Printed by Mathew Carey, no. 118, Market-Street,, 1794), Sermon IV.

xliii See chapter three, "Your Life's Message, Will, and Testament," in Robert Davis Smart, *Legacy from Christ: What's My Message?* (Bloomington, IN: WestBow, 2017), pp. 37-54.

xliv Sereno E. Dwight, "Memoirs of Jonathan Edwards," *Works, 1:clxxviii*

xlv *Ibid.*, 1:clxxix

Made in the USA
Monee, IL
23 March 2021

62832067R00105